Games That Time Forgot

Games That Time Forgot

A guide to over 100 obscure 19th and early 20th parlor games

Adam Shefts

To order additional copies of this book, contact:
Xlibris
1-888-795-4274
www.Xlibris.com
Orders@Xlibris.com
803055

CONTENTS

Tea-Pot
Twenty Questions
Up Jenkins
What is My Thought Like?

Happy Jumps
Raisin Race
Three Tin Cups
True Lover Test

Boots Without Shoes
Clairvoyant
The Farmyard
An Impossible Jump
Kissing the Candlestick
Make a Card Dance Upon the Wall
Mesmerizing
Obstacles
The Sorcerer Behind the Screen
Wooden Face

"Would you like to give
our games a shot?
You can, with
GAMES THAT TIME FORGOT"

PREFACE

Prior to conducting research for this book, I was not aware of most of the games I would eventually come across. I had not heard of many of these games nor variations of them. As an enthusiast of the Victorian and Edwardian eras and an avid researcher of all things obscure and unusual related to these periods in American history, these games had somehow eluded me through the years. How had I not known about these games which once entertained so many households well over a century ago? My research for this book led me down an interesting path into a form of entertainment no longer common.

Time waits for nothing. It marches on, taking with it information it deems necessary for future generations to know. For other information not deemed necessary to know, time forgets. The content between the covers of this book is one such example. Time marched on; these games did not. Once played so lively by the young and the old, these games slowly disappeared with the passing of each individual who once played and enjoyed them so heartily. As a result, these games fell further and further into obscurity with each passing year, so much so, that even with information so readily available today at our fingertips, many of these games cannot be found online. Time marched on and left these games behind; lost and forgotten. Until now.

My research for this book came in the form of sifting through books and periodicals of the 19th and early 20th century. Some of these books and periodicals are from my personal collection. Others I had come across at antique shops and though too expensive to purchase, still aided me in my research. You may be asking why there aren't more games appearing in this book, when game books of the time typically each contained over 100 games.

The answer is simple. There is no need to publish a book of games in which many of those games can be found online. Many games within the books I used for research can easily be searched and found. These easily found games are not ones I wanted in this book. I wanted this book to contain as many games as I could come across which could not easily be found in a general online search, if they could be found online at all. This required many hours of taking games found in books and conducting a search for those games online using game titles (which varied over the years), key words and game descriptions. If attempting to locate those games provided enough of a challenge, those were games I wanted in this book. The exception to this is Blind Man's Buff, a game very easily found on many websites. However, due to its immense popularity, it is one of those games no publication on 19th and early 20th century entertainment would be complete without. Another game which can easily be found online is Telephone, which happens to be just one the game's many names. However, it is included in this book as it's interesting to note how far this game dates back.

Many gameplay instructions within the books I used for research were written in a now antiquated manner, using terms no longer applied to modern English. I therefore took liberties of rewriting all game instructions in a more modern style for all to understand and easily follow should anyone wish to play these games.

This leads me to mention that not all games within this book are safe or appropriate to play. Some games involve the use of fire indoors, such as Snap-Dragon and Jack's Alive. Others, such as Kissing the Candlestick, involve tricking someone into being kissed. Then there are games such as Here I Bake, which could potentially lead to injuries. Many of the games in this book are harmless but for those which have the potential to be harmful, whether physically or emotionally, player discretion is advised. Use judgment. Any player who chooses to play a game from this book which has the potential for injury, property damage or lawsuits do so at their own risk.

Parlor games would sometimes include forfeits. Forfeits were penalties players would rack up throughout a game in which they had to pay those forfeits afterward, usually in some embarrassing challenge. There were two ways of playing parlor games. One way involved the elimination of players who either provided an incorrect answer to a question, made an error, was unable to complete a task within a certain amount of time, etc. The other way, using forfeits, allowed players to remain in a game rather than be eliminated, resulting in racking up forfeits, or penalties, for the actions mentioned above which would otherwise result in an elimination. When the game ended, each player had to pay however many forfeits they accumulated during the game by performing one challenge per forfeit, the challenge selected by the game leader. Numerous lists of forfeits can easily be found online or you may make up your own. For this book, I've chosen to go the route of player elimination, which actually works better for a number of these games, as winners are determined in many of them by players being eliminated.

These games are a part of the legacy previous generations have left us. They deserve to be brought back, to be given a second chance to be enjoyed by current and future generations. Let's allow the spirit of these games to once again hear the shouts of joy and laughter and the simple pleasures of family and friends gathering together to enjoy these games as others had so long ago.

Adam Shefts
Gettysburg, PA
September, 2019

ACKNOWLEDGEMENT

Many thanks go out to all those who offered encouragement and advice during the writing of this book. Though research and writing this book was a joy in itself, the support and shared excitement by many regarding this book, from its conception to its publishing, made the experience all that more enjoyable. Know that your support and encouragement helped make this book possible.

INTRODUCTION

"At merry Christmas-time, or on a wet day in the country, or in the city too, for that matter, or on a winter's evening, when the fire is burning cheerily, pussy purring on the hearth, and the lamps lighted, young folks are often at a loss, and their elders too, sometimes, to know how to amuse themselves. Some people will say, "There are books, let them read." We would whisper in their ears an adage as old as the hills, but none the less true or pithy; It is this: "All work and no play makes Jack a dull boy." And again, let us remember that we also were once young, and laughed as heartily over "Blind Man's Buff" as the youngest of our acquaintance. All the apparatus required in parlor games is good temper, good spirits, and gentleness, so that at any moment amusement for an evening can be obtained by anybody who wills it."

The above paragraph, so eloquently stated, is the introduction to *Fireside Games; A Repertory of Social Amusements*, published in 1859. It is just one of a number of books I used in compiling the collection of over 100 games you are now holding and perusing.

When one today thinks of games, it is often associated with technology. Gaming systems and phone apps have long since replaced the days when games were born of the imagination, when rooms were filled with the laughter of game participants and observers, allowing for the creation of memories to fondly recall many years later.

Parlor games may seem antiquated by today's standards but as another adage goes, "Everything old is new again". My goal in writing this book was to find the most obscure, if not completely forgotten, parlor games of the 19th and early 20th century and share them with a new generation of potential players, allowing life to be breathed into these games once more. My hope is for you, the reader, to resurrect these games from the hands of time and enjoy them among family and friends, as others did so many years and generations ago.

Now put down your phones, turn off the television and close your laptops. Let's play some parlor games!

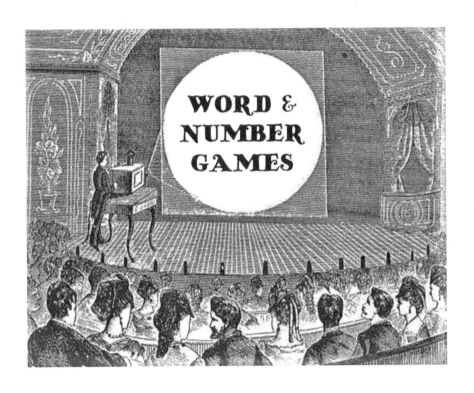

WORD &
NUMBER
GAMES

Alphabet Minute

This game is played in the format of a conversation and requires quick thinking as players are required to immediately keep the conversation going, each player's contribution to the conversation beginning with the next letter of the alphabet as per the example below.

To begin, all players form a circle, either seated or standing. The conversation then begins as the following example among four players demonstrates:

Player 1: "All the leaves are changing color."

Player 2: "Before you know it, winter will be here."

Player 3: "Can't autumn stay a bit longer?"

Player 4: "Don't like winter?"

Player 1: "Extremely cold temperatures are not my thing."

Player 2: "Forget the negative aspects of winter and let's focus on the positives."

Player 3: "Going to try skiing for the first time this winter."

Player 4: "Hadn't you tried it last year?"

Player 1: "I was going to but something came up and I had to postpone it."

Player 2: "Just reminded me, when is that postponed dinner being rescheduled?"

Player 3: "Knowing would be helpful as my calendar is filling up fast."

Player 4: "Let's schedule it soon."

Etc, etc.

As you can see, Player 1 started the conversation with a question beginning with the letter A. Player 2 then contributed with a sentence beginning with the letter B. Player 3 then began a sentence with the letter C and so on down the alphabet.

Though the example given starts with a question beginning with the letter A, the game may start with a sentence rather than a question and doesn't need to begin with the letter A. The game may begin with any letter of the alphabet just as long as every player's contribution begins with the next letter of the alphabet. Reaching the letter Z, the game would naturally continue on starting from A (the letter X may be omitted). The game may cover an array of topics as long as the topics are segued into as the above example demonstrated, with a skiing trip having been postponed reminding a player of a postponed dinner.

If a player is unable to think quickly and stalls, that player is eliminated. The player lasting the longest who does not stall in keeping the conversation going is the winner.

Buzz

Those strong at math will likely find this game more enjoyable than those who are not strong in the subject. Players form a circle and begin to count in turn, starting from 1, but must substitute the word "Buzz" in place of any number in which 7 appears or any number in which there is a multiple of 7.

Let's suppose, for example, that players have already counted around the circle from 1 through 6. The next player would say "Buzz". Then counting would continue around the circle from 8 through 13. The next player, rather than saying 14, would say "Buzz" because 7 multiplied by 2 is 14. The next two players would say 15 and 16. The player after would say "Buzz" instead of 17. Counting would then continue from 18 through 20. The next player, would say "Buzz" instead of 21 because 7 multiplied by 3 is 21. If any player forgets to say "Buzz" in place of any number containing 7 or containing a multiple of 7, that player is eliminated.

Capping Verses

All players sit around a table and are handed a sheet of paper and a pencil. At the top of the sheet, each player writes a single line of poetry, whether original or one from memory. Once that line is written, it is folded back and out of sight and passed to the player on the right. The player to receive the sheet cannot see what the previous line is, as it's been folded back. However, they must be told by the person passing the paper to them what the last word they wrote was. Based on the last word, the player now writes their own line of poetry, which again can either be original or from memory. The last word they write must rhyme with the previous last word they were told of. That player's line of poetry, like the first, is then folded back and out of sight, to be passed again to the player on the right in which that player must be told what the new last word written was. This continues among all players until the papers have gone around the table once or twice, each player having had the opportunity to write a line or two of poetry, depending on how many times the papers have gone around. Each player then takes turns unfolding the paper they have in front of them and reads aloud the mishmash of poetry created on each one.

Cupid

One player chosen to be the leader stands at one side of the room while all other players stand on the other side. If the leader is male, he will be Jupiter. If female, she will be Venus. The other players will all be Cupid. One by one, the Cupids must state an adjective and approach Jupiter/Venus in the manner which is expressed by that adjective. The adjectives must go in alphabetical order starting from A.

For example, the first Cupid, representing the letter A, may announce "Cupid comes Acting", in which that player will then proceed to walk across the room toward Jupiter/Venus in a theatrical manner. The next Cupid, representing the letter B, may say, "Cupid comes Barking" and then proceeds to bark like a dog while approaching Jupiter/Venus. The next player, representing the letter C, may say, "Cupid comes Crawling", and then proceeds to crawl across the room to Jupiter/Venus. The game continues in this manner throughout the alphabet (the letter X may be omitted). Each player returns to the starting position upon their turn being completed to be ready for their next turn with whichever letter in the alphabet they will now represent. Once the letter Z has been reached, the alphabet starts over again from the letter A. If any player cannot think of an adjective upon their turn or repeats an adjective already used, they are eliminated.

Earth, Air and Water or The Elements

Players are seated in a circle around one player standing in the center who holds a handkerchief rolled up into a ball. The player standing in the center then tosses the handkerchief ball into another player's lap while simultaneously saying either "earth", "air" or "water". Whoever's lap the handkerchief ball lands in must name an animal associated with that element but they must do so before the player who threw the handkerchief counts to ten. Counting begins as soon as the handkerchief hits the player's lap. Counting may be done quickly to add additional excitement to the game.

For example, if the player standing throws the handkerchief ball into someone's lap while saying "earth", the player whose lap the handkerchief lands in may say "horse", "dog", "giraffe", etc. before the count of ten is up. If "water" is said, a player may answer "fish", "octopus", "dolphin", etc. Both general and specific names can be used. For instance, even if a player says "fish", another player can say "goldfish" or "salmon". The name of an animal, whether general or specific, cannot be used more than once per game. Those who either cannot come up with the name of an animal within the count of ten, names a wrong animal for the element or repeats the name of an animal already given is eliminated.

Famous Numbers

Players are seated around a table. Each player is provided ten slips of paper and writes a number upon each one ranging from 1 through 100 (it's okay if the same number is written by multiple players). The slips of paper are then collected and put into a bag or box and shaken up. One by one, each player pulls out a number, reads it to the others and must name something or someone associated with that number without too much hesitation. For instance, if a player selects the number 3, they may say "Babe Ruth", who wore the number 3. Saying something associated with the last two numbers of a year is allowable. Say, for instance, the number 63 is selected, that player may say "the battle of Gettysburg", which occurred in 1863 or "the assassination of JFK", which occurred in 1963. Anything or anyone may be named in association with a number. If too much hesitation is taken to name something or someone associated with a number or if a player repeats something already said by another, if that same number was previously picked, that player is eliminated.

The Forbidden Letter

The idea of this game is to not use a certain letter in anything said.

All players form a circle and decide on a topic to discuss and a letter not to use. For example, the topic is vacation and the letter "M" cannot be used. Each player takes a turn answering and asking a question, omitting the letter M as per the example below:

Player 1 to Player 2 on his/her left: "If you could go anywhere on vacation, where would it be?" (There is no letter M used in this question. This question was asked correctly).

Player 2 answers Player 1: "I would go to Italy for a few weeks." (Notice how the words "a few weeks" were used in place of "a month", which contains the letter M. Player 2 answered the question correctly).

Player 2 then asks Player 3: "Vacations always go by too quick, don't they?" (Again, no letter M is used).

Player 3 responds: "Yes they do. There is never enough time."

Player 3 used the word "time", containing the letter M. He/she is therefore eliminated. Player 4 then resumes the game by asking a question to Player 5, who will answer Player 4 before asking a question to Player 6 and so on around the circle. If either a question or answer contains the forbidden letter, that player is eliminated. Questions and answers must be spoken without hesitation. If a player hesitates too long, that is also cause for elimination. The winner is the last remaining individual who does not use the forbidden letter or hesitate too long in answering or asking a question.

I Love My Love With an "A"

Players form a circle. The goal of the game is for each player to recite, without too much hesitation, a love, hate, name, location and gift, each item beginning with the appropriate letter of the alphabet they represent depending on when their turn occurs, as demonstrated in the example below.

Player 1: "I love my love with an "A", because she is Adorable; I hate her with an "A" because she is Annoying. Her name is Allison, she comes from Atlanta and I gave her an Apple.

Player 2: "I love my love with a "B" because he is Bold; I hate him with a "B" because he is Bitter. His name is Bill, he comes from Buffalo and I gave him a Baseball.

Player 3: "I love my love with a "C" because she is Cute; I hate her with a "C" because she is Cunning. Her name is Carol, she comes from Cincinnati and I gave her Candy.

The next player would start with a D, the next with an E and so on through the alphabet, starting again from A once Z has been reached (the letter X may be omitted). The names spoken by each player do not have to be the names of someone that player may actually know. This game is not about loving or hating someone you know but rather how quick and imaginative one can be under the pressure of time.

Words, names, locations and items cannot be used more than once per game, if the game happens to last long enough to begin over again from "A". If a player hesitates for too long on any item or repeats a name or item already used (should the game, again, happen to go on long enough to begin again from the start of the alphabet), that player is eliminated. As more and more players are eliminated, which will minimize the amount of time between turns, those still involved in it will find the game becomes more challenging as they will have less and less time in planning ahead what to say for the next letter they represent.

The Minister's Cat

All players form a circle. The first player starts the game by describing the minister's cat with an adjective beginning with the letter A. For example, Player 1 may say "The minister's cat is an adorable cat". Player 2 may then say "The minister's cat is an adventurous cat". This continues around the circle at a rapid pace until it gets back to Player 1, at which point adjectives will then begin with the letter B, the rapid pace not being broken during the transition to the next letter. Player 1 may say, "The minister's cat is a beautiful cat". Player 2 then may say "The minister's cat is a bashful cat", and so on around the circle. Each time the game comes full circle back to Player 1, adjectives describing the minister's cat will begin with the next letter of the alphabet, but always excluding the letter X. If a player cannot come up with an adjective beginning with the appropriate letter or repeats an adjective already used, that player is eliminated. Gameplay continues in this manner until only one player is left, becoming the winner.

The Schoolmaster

One player is chosen to be the schoolmaster and stands or sits on one side of the room. All other players are pupils and stand or sit facing the schoolmaster, lined up one behind the other as if in a classroom. The object of this game is for the pupils to try to obtain a place at the front of the line and remain there for as long as possible, thereby being the head of the class. The first pupil who happens to be at the start of the line once the game begins doesn't necessarily mean they will stay there.

The schoolmaster, starting with the first pupil in line, asks for the name of something beginning with a certain letter of the alphabet. For example, the schoolmaster may ask, "What is a name of a bird beginning with the letter F?" or "What is a food beginning with the letter M?"

That pupil must provide an answer before the schoolmaster counts to ten. If an appropriate answer is provided, that pupil remains where they are in line. If an answer cannot be provided before the count of ten is up, the same question then goes to the next pupil in line. If that pupil provides an appropriate response, they then move ahead of the pupil in front of them who was not able to provide one. Gameplay continues in this manner down the line until the last pupil is reached, at which point the schoolmaster returns to the beginning of the line. Though the schoolmaster may ask the same question more than once throughout the game, the same responses cannot be provided by the pupils. If a response already provided by one pupil is again provided by another, it is to be treated the same as not providing a response within a count of ten and so the question then goes to the next pupil, who has a chance to respond differently. If that pupil responds appropriately within the count of ten, he/she moves ahead of the pupil in front of them.

There is no completion of this game. It continues on for as long as players wish. The image below, though demonstrating the positions to be taken by the schoolmaster and pupils, is slightly inaccurate, as all of the pupils should be arranged in a single line, one behind the other.

The Story Game

This is not so much a game as it is a simple group activity involving imagination.

The object is to tell a made-up story in parts, each player leaving off at an exciting point in the story, which is to immediately be picked up and continued by the next player and so on down the line until the story is completed by the last player.

For example, Player 1 begins:

"There was a man walking down the street minding his own business when a dog came racing toward him, bearing its teeth. As the dog got closer, the man froze in place, preparing himself for the attack. Thirty feet, twenty feet, now just ten feet away, the man turned to run but the dog lunged, grabbing a hold of his coat, when suddenly —"

Player 2 then immediately picks up where Player 1 left off: "—a bee stung the dog's leg. Panicked with pain, the dog gave up its attack on the man and began running around carelessly, knocking a child off his bike, getting a girl's new dress wet as it ran through a puddle and causing other forms of havoc. With the pain eventually subsiding, the dog turned its attention back toward the man it had originally gone after but just as it did —"

The next player would immediately continue the story, leaving off at another cliffhanger for the next player to continue from. The last player in the game is to finish the story. The story can go in any direction the players wish and can be as creative as their imaginations allow.

Telephone

This is a game many may already be familiar with. Players form a circle and one starts the game by whispering to his/her neighbor any sentence they wish. That person in turn then whispers the same exact sentence to their neighbor, who whispers it to theirs and so on around the circle until it gets back to the person who started the whisper. The person who started it then tells everyone what the sentence they originally whispered was and what sentence was just whispered to them by the last player in the circle. On many occasions, the original sentence whispered will be inadvertently altered on its way around the circle, coming back differently to the original player who whispered it.

Word Making

Each player is provided a sheet of paper and pencil. One player chooses a long word which everyone has to write down. For example, the word "Mediterranean" is chosen and written down. Starting from the first letter M, all players must make as many words as they can out of "Mediterranean" beginning with that letter. Each letter can only be used once to make other words unless that letter appears more than once. For example, the letter D cannot be used more than once as it only appears one time in "Mediterranean" but the letter E may be used three times as it appears that many times in the word. A time limit of five minutes is allowed to do this. When time is up, each player reads aloud the words they were able to come up with out of "Mediterranean" beginning with the letter M. If a player has come up with a word which no other player has come up with, that player is awarded a point. The game then continues on in the same manner with the next letter of the word "Mediterranean", this being the letter E. The game ends when all letters in the word have been played. In the case a word contains the same letter more than once, such as in the example of "Mediterranean", duplicate letters are omitted. Therefore, after the first time making words out of "Mediterranean" beginning with the letter E, players do not have to come up with words beginning with that letter again. Sticking with the example of "Mediterranean", the game would have eight rounds, in which players would have to make up words beginning with letters M, E, D, I, T, R, A and N. The player with the most points at the end of the game, that is, whoever had come up with the most words no one else did within each five-minute round, is the winner.

Apple and Candle

A string is suspended from the ceiling or a light fixture with the lower end secured around the stem of an apple. A candle is then stuck into the side of the apple. The apple should be hanging at a height in which everyone can easily reach it with their mouth. The candle is then lit and the apple is spun while given a push so that as the apple swings back and forth, the candle is rotating. Players take turns attempting to catch the swinging apple by their teeth without getting burned by the lit candle. If the swinging momentum slows down, the apple is to be spun while pushed again. No other method of capturing the apple may be used other than players' mouths. The player who safely catches the apple in their teeth wins the game, and the apple. This was a popular game at Halloween, accompanied by other games involving apples such as Bobbing for Apples or Bobbing for Apples with a Fork, which appears in this book.

Apple and Candle resulted in many injuries as it was not uncommon while attempting to catch the swinging apple by their teeth that players accidentally caught the candle, burning their mouths. A safer variation of this game in the early 20th century involved swapping a lit candle for a small bag of flour secured to the side of the apple. Rather than potentially biting onto a lit candle, a player may instead be hit in the face with the flour bag, their face potentially becoming marked with spots of flour.

Are You There, Moriarty?

Two players are blindfolded, given a rolled-up newspaper and kneel down opposite one another while clasping each other's hand. The first player asks, "Are you there, Moriarty?" to which his or her opponent replies, "Yes Sir/Ma'am, I am here!" Player 1 then has to try to blindly hit Player 2 in the head or torso with the newspaper, judging where he/she is only by the sound of their voice. Player 2 may try to dodge the blow, but their knees must remain in place on the floor at all times and clasped hands cannot come apart. Player 2 then asks, "Are you there, Moriarty?" and attempts to hit Player 1 upon his/her response in the same manner. The two players continue taking turns asking the question, providing the answer and swinging the newspaper. The winner is the first to reach a certain number of hits on the other's head or torso.

Gameplay rules changed by the early 20th century in which players' knees were allowed to leave the ground in order to roll out of the way of a hit, though both players' hands must still remained clasped, unlike what is depicted in the following image, with hands unclasped.

The Blind Feeding the Blind

Two people are blindfolded and kneel on the floor facing each other. Each is given a spoon of some type of dry food in which they must try to feed it to the other. It is best to put a towel on the floor for easy cleanup. If it is decided soft foods or sauces/liquids be used, it is best for the participants to cover up their clothing as the game could get messy. There are no points awarded or eliminations in this game. It is really for the enjoyment of the spectators to watch the two participants blindly and sloppily trying to feed each other.

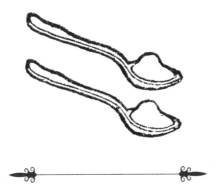

Blind Man's Buff

A large room is ideal for this game as lots of movement is involved. A player is selected to be the blind man (or woman, though women involved in this game during its popularity were still referred to as the blind man). The player selected to be the blind man is blindfolded and then spun around three times. The blind man must then try to catch someone in the room. Players are to move around to avoid being caught and may even distract the blind man into heading in a different direction. Touching the blind man is not permitted. Upon being caught, the blind man must correctly identify whom he/she has captured. If guessed correctly, the player caught now becomes the blind man, is spun around three times, and the game continues on. If guessed incorrectly, the current blindfolded player remains the blind man.

Blowing Out the Candle

A candle is lit and placed on a table. One person is then blindfolded and spun around three times to disorient them. That person then must try to blow out the candle, which often results in them blowing in a different direction than where the candle is located, providing amusement for those watching.

Bobbing for Apples with a Fork

Bobbing for apples dates back to the Roman invasion of Britain in 43 AD, the Roman army celebrating the success of their invasion with a festival and games. By the late 19th century, bobbing for apples, though still a popular activity, especially at Halloween, needed a little spicing up after being played the same way for nearly 2,000 years. Thus, a fork was introduced to the game, not only adding a different degree of difficulty but also making it a little more sanitary for those concerned with germs.

Players make a circle around a tub filled with water and containing apples. Unlike the traditional game of bobbing for apples, all players are to remain standing in this game. One by one, players take a fork, placing the end of the handle between their teeth, then lining up the fork with an apple in the tub. When that player feels the fork is properly aligned with an apple, they release it from their teeth, the fork falling and hopefully sticking into one. If successful, that apple is removed from the tub and that player may either remove themselves from the game, having already successfully caught an apple, or they may remain in an attempt to catch another one when their turn comes around again. Players are only allowed one chance per turn to successfully get a fork to stick into an apple. If the fork dropped is way off mark, that player may not try again until their turn in the rotation comes back around. The game continues until all apples have been caught in this manner. There are no points or eliminations in this game. It is merely a fun activity for all to partake in.

Bullet and Bracelet

A bracelet is suspended by a string in the center of the room either from the ceiling or a light fixture. A piece of tin foil is rolled into a ball (the bullet) no larger than a grape. One by one, each player attempts to throw the bullet through the bracelet, standing at least 8-10 feet away from the bracelet. The first player to successfully throw the bullet through the bracelet ten times, or however many number of times decided upon, is the winner.

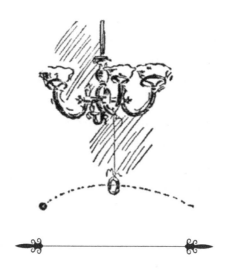

Change Seats

Like Musical Chairs, the game of Change Seats requires one less chair than there are players. Players are seated on chairs in a circle with one player standing in the center of that circle. The player standing asks one of the seated players, "Do you love your neighbor?" That seated player may either say yes, in which the players to either side of him/her remain seated or the player may say no, in which the players on either side of him/her must jump up and quickly change seats before the player standing steals one of the seats for him/herself. Therefore, you have three players attempting to claim two vacant seats. Whichever player does not get a seat will now be the one standing in the center of the circle asking the question, "Do you love your neighbor?", resulting in the previously described responses and actions.

Upon being asked if someone loves their neighbor, a player may also say, for example, "Yes, except one who has blue eyes", "Yes, except one who plays a musical instrument", "Yes, except one whose birthday falls in July", etc. Players may get as creative as they want with their responses and all other seated players who fit the criteria must jump up and quickly change seats before the player standing can grab one of them, causing a new, or possibly the same player if not quick enough to grab a vacant seat, to become or remain the one standing asking, "Do you love your neighbor?"

There is no completion to this game as seats are never removed like they are in Musical Chairs. The game continues on for as long as players wish. Though other games pre-dating Change Seats posed a risk of injury and/or property damage, such as Blind Man's Buff, Change Seats was one of the only parlor games in which safety precautions were recommended. It was advised that all valuables and good furniture be removed from the playing area as the game could become chaotic at times.

Cotton Flies

All players sit in a very close circle. One player starts the game by tossing up a piece of cotton (a small light feather may be used as well) and blowing it into the air toward another player. The player the piece of cotton is heading toward must not let it fall in his/her lap, therefore blowing it away. The object of the game is for all players to blow the piece of cotton and keep it afloat, not letting the cotton fall in their lap. If the cotton falls in a player's lap, that player receives a strike against them. Just like in baseball, after three strikes, that player is eliminated. The last player remaining in the game, in which the cotton has not landed on them three times, is the winner.

The Deer and the Hunter

This game is played by only two players at a time. One player represents a deer and the other a hunter. Both players are blindfolded and placed at opposite ends of a table. All other players are to stand off to the side while one is designated to be a timekeeper (another player will need to take over as timekeeper when it is the designated timekeeper's turn to play). The object of the game is for the hunter to capture the deer and for the deer to avoid being caught for as long as possible. In doing so, both players are to run around the table, using only the sound of their opponent to gauge where they are located. If and when the hunter captures the deer, the timekeeper writes down how long it took for the deer to be captured. The players then swap roles, the hunter now becoming the deer and the deer becoming the hunter. Once both players have had turns being both the deer and the hunter and upon both being captured as the deer, in which the timekeeper is keeping track of how long it took each to be captured, two new players become the deer and hunter, continuing gameplay in the same manner. Once everyone in the game has had a turn of being the deer and the hunter and all deer have been captured, the game is then over. The timekeeper will then review the list of times it took for each deer to be captured. The player, as the deer, who escaped capture for the longest period of time is the winner.

Ennui

Ennui is another word for boredom. In this game, the game leader yawns, attempting to get the other players to yawn as well, as the act of yawning can be contagious. Each player who yawns is eliminated. The game leader may yawn as much as he/she wants until all players except one have yawned, the one remaining who hasn't yawned becoming the winner.

The Extinguisher

One player lights a candle. The other players line up, one behind the other, facing the player holding the candle. One by one, the player holding the candle rapidly passes it by the first player's nose. As the candle rapidly passes by, that player attempts to blow it out. The candle is to be passed by each player's nose only once. If unsuccessful, that player then moves to the back of the line to await their next turn, giving the next player in line a chance to blow out the candle in the same manner. As it can prove difficult to blow out a candle moving rapidly, the first person to successfully blow it out is the winner.

Fan Race

This game was mainly played by ladies but gentlemen may participate as well. All players stand in a row, side by side, on one side of the room. A finish line is established at the other side. Players are given a handheld fan and a piece of cotton is placed on the floor in front of each one. At the signal to begin, players begin fanning the piece of cotton in front of them, the air produced by the fan pushing the cotton toward the finish line. The player whose piece of cotton crosses the finish line first wins. As fanning may cause erratic movements of the cotton, it is likely players will need to chase after it in different directions and fan it back on course during the race, adding unpredictability and excitement to the game.

Five

Players sit on one side of a room while a person on the other side (the thrower) stands holding a knotted handkerchief. The thrower tosses the handkerchief to any player sitting across the room. As soon as the handkerchief makes contact with an individual, the thrower counts aloud to five, in which the player now holding the handkerchief must name an object that is round. The count of five should be rapid, done in around three seconds. If a player names an object that is round within the count of five, they remain seated and throw the handkerchief back to the thrower, to be thrown to someone else, or to that same person again if the thrower wishes. If a player cannot name a round object within the count of five, no elimination occurs but that player exchanges places with the thrower and now becomes the one tossing the handkerchief. Once a round object has been named, that object cannot be mentioned again during the game. Any player who repeats the name of a round object already mentioned is eliminated. Eliminations will eventually come rapidly as the game progresses and players find it difficult coming up with new round objects to name. The last person remaining seated is the winner.

The difficulty of this game can be increased by the thrower starting their count to five as soon as the handkerchief is released so that by the time it reaches a seated player, the count is already up to three, giving that player barely any time to name a round object and therefore possibly leading to an object being repeated, resulting in quicker eliminations.

Flicking the Cork

A table is set up against a wall. On the table is placed a wine bottle with the cork resting atop the bottle, not pushed in. With the combined height of the table and the wine bottle, the cork should be about four feet off the floor. Though a wine bottle was often used, any other tall slender item may be used in its place, or the cork may be placed upon a wall-mounted candle holder as depicted in the following image. Either way, the cork should again be about four feet off the floor. Players line up in a row, one behind the other, with at least two feet of distance between each one. All players outstretch one arm and begin walking, one behind the other, as fast as they can in a circle around the room. As each player passes by the cork, they attempt to flick it off the wine bottle. The game is tougher than it appears as all players must keep an outstretched arm and walk as quickly as possible around the room the entire game. The combination of keeping an arm outstretched while keeping a rapid walking pace often results in players flicking a little high, missing the cork over a number of passes around the room. The first player to successfully flick the cork off the bottle is the winner. Players may not swat or slap the cork off. It must be flicked off with the finger and thumb. A player, designated the umpire, watches all players to make sure all keep their arm completely outstretched without any bend in it, as a slightly bent arm will make flicking the cork easier, which is cheating. The umpire will also watch to make sure players aren't slowing down their pace as they near the cork in order to get better aim, which is also cheating. Once the cork is flicked off, that player is pronounced the winner. The cork is then reset atop the bottle, a new umpire is chosen, and the game begins anew.

Here I Bake

Players stand in a circle, joining hands to create a ring. One player, the baker, stands in the center of that ring. The object is for the baker to get out of the ring by breaking through those creating it.

The baker walks around inside the ring, touching joined hands as he/she goes around. At the first joined hands touched, the baker says "Here I bake". Continuing to go around the ring, the baker touches another pair of joined hands, saying "Here I brew". Another pair of joined hands are yet touched, the baker saying "Here I make my wedding cake". With the fourth and last pair of joined hands touched, the baker says "And here I mean to break through". With those last words, the baker makes a dash through the joined hands he/she had just touched, attempting to escape. If successful, the player whose hand broke away first, allowing the baker to escape, becomes the baker in the next game. If the players successfully hold the baker from breaking through, that person remains the baker and must once again go through the words and actions described above. Those interested in playing this game do so at their own risk as injuries may possibly occur.

Jack's Alive

Players form a circle. A piece of firewood is put into a lit fireplace until one end of it ignites. One player then immediately takes the firewood out and blows out the fire so the firewood now contains only embers. That player then says "Jack's alive" and passes the firewood onto the next player who must immediately upon receiving the firewood also say "Jack's alive" before passing it to the next who immediately repeats the same words, and so on around the circle. The object of the game is for each player to receive the firewood and hand it off to the next player as quickly as possible before the embers burn out. Whichever player is holding the firewood at the time the embers burn out is eliminated. A player is also eliminated if they don't immediately say "Jack's alive" upon receiving the firewood.

Jinglers

All players except one are blindfolded. The player not blindfolded (the bell holder) moves around the room while holding a bell (or has a bell hung around his/her neck). As the bell holder moves around, the bell will naturally ring in which the blindfolded players, guided only by the sound of the bell, must try to catch the bell holder. The first blindfolded player to catch the bell holder becomes the bell holder in the next game. Caution should be taken as all blindfolded players will be running in the same direction simultaneously.

One-Legged Lefties

This game was so named due to it being believed that things were more difficult to accomplish with the left side of the body than with the right. However, this game may prove equally as challenging no matter which knee or hand is used. Players are divided into teams of two so that everyone has a partner. A timekeeper is selected (another player will need to take over as timekeeper when it is the designated timekeeper's turn to play). One team playing at a time, partners kneel on the floor facing each other. Both players are provided a candle in which one candle is lit. Though the game's name suggests balancing on the left knee, players may balance on the right if they wish but whichever knee they balance on, they must hold the candle in the hand on the same side. If balancing on the left knee, the candle is held in the left hand. The same goes for the right side.

Using the left knee as an example, both players are to balance on their left knee while holding their right foot with their right hand, as depicted in the image below. Attempting to keep their balance, they are to touch candles so that the lit candle lights the unlit one. Once lit, the timekeeper notes how long it took for that team to light the unlit candle. One candle is then blown out, both candles then being handed to the next team. After all teams have had a turn, whichever team lit the unlit candle in the shortest amount of time is the winning team.

It is advised playing this game on a thick rug or placing a pad beneath the knee being balanced on in order to avoid knee injuries.

Optical Game

A thin stick must be gathered from outside, measuring at least 2 feet long and should be crooked to make this game more challenging. A ring is also needed which must have a flat edge so that it can be stood upright. A player is selected to be the timekeeper (another player will need to take over as timekeeper when it is the designated timekeeper's turn to play). The ring is stood up on a table in which one by one, players must close one eye and try to pass the stick through the upright ring. By closing one eye, it increases the difficulty of performing this task. If the ring is accidentally knocked over, it must immediately be set back up again so as not to waste any time in attempting to pass the stick through it. Once each player has had a turn to pass the crooked stick through the ring with one eye closed, the timekeeper will review the times it took for each player to successfully complete the task. The player who did it in the least amount of time is the winner.

Oranges and Lemons

This game originated in England but as many American customs were adopted from England during the 19th century, including forms of entertainment, this game found its way to the United States. Two players are chosen to be team leaders. The leaders decide secretly amongst each other which they will represent, oranges or lemons. The two leaders then stand facing each other, their hands meeting in the middle above their heads so they themselves create an arch. On the floor between them should be a dividing line made of tape or any other item which cannot be easily kicked or moved. The other players form a line, each one holding the waist or shirt of the person in front of them as they walk single file beneath the arch created by the two leaders. The line of players continues to circle around in order to keep passing through the arch. As the players pass through the arch, the two leaders recite the following:

"Oranges and lemons,
Say the bells of St. Clement's;
You owe me five farthings,
Say the bells of St. Martin's;
When will you pay me?
Say the bells of Old Bailey.
When I grow rich,

Say the bells of Shoreditch.
When will that be?
Say the bells of Stepney.
I do not know,
Says the great bell of Bow.
Here comes a candle to light you to bed,
Here comes the chopper to chop off your head!
Chip chop chip chop the last man's dead!"

    If the leaders are unable to memorize this rhyme, it may be posted on a wall or this book may be held by one of the leaders for them to read aloud from while still completing the arch with one hand. At the last word, "dead", the leaders are to bring their hands down in order to trap the player who happens to be walking beneath the arch at that moment. That player is then asked by one of the leaders, "Oranges or Lemons?", to which that player must make a choice, his/her answer to be whispered so that none of the other players can hear and know which leader represents which fruit. Depending on their answer, that player is to then stand behind the leader representing either oranges or lemons and grab a hold of that leader's waist. Gameplay then resumes, with another player again being stopped beneath the arch when the last word, "dead", is spoken. That player, like the previous, will whisper either oranges or lemons and then stand behind the leader representing whichever fruit they decided upon, or stand behind other players in line if there are already others behind that leader. All players in line are to grab a hold of the waste of the person in front of them. Once all players have been assigned to a line depending on their choice of oranges or lemons, and with the leaders' hands still clasped together, a game of tug-of-war ensues, hence why players will need to hang onto each other. Whichever side pulls all the players from the other across the dividing line first is the winning team.

Patchwork

Prior to the game beginning, as many photographs as there are players will be needed. Each photograph is to be cut once vertically and once horizontally to create four rectangular pieces of the same size. One piece of each photo is then set aside while the other three pieces of each photo are put into a box and shaken up. Players are to sit around a table in which the box of photograph pieces are placed in the center of it. Each player around the table is presented with the one piece of each photo initially put aside. The object of the game is for players to locate the other three pieces of their photo, to be put together as a jigsaw puzzle would. At the signal to begin the game, all players simultaneously reach into the box to find the other three matching pieces needed to complete their photo. The first player to put together the rest of their photo wins. This is a short game but could be rather chaotic with the flurry of players' hands all reaching into the box simultaneously in a race to find the needed pieces of their photograph. To increase the difficulty of this game, additional vertical and horizontal cuts to photos may be made, creating more pieces.

The Race

One player is given five ordinary crackers and another is given a small glass of water and a spoon. At a given signal, the player with the crackers begins eating them one at a time while the player with the water begins drinking it with the spoon as if slurping soup. The cracker-eater cannot have any beverage to assist him/her in swallowing the dry crackers and the water-drinker cannot touch the glass to his/her lips, using only the spoon. Whoever finishes first, the crackers or the water, wins.

Reverend Crawley's Game

This game typically consists of between eight and ten players. Players stand in a circle and hold hands but not with the person next to them and both hands cannot be held by the same person. As a result, there will be a tangled web of arms which players have to try to untangle without letting go of the hands they're holding. This requires lots of twisting and maneuvering in which all players will eventually become untangled and back in the starting circle, or two separate circles depending on whose hands they're holding.

This game was popular among singles as it involves lots of physical contact.

Rule of Contrary

Each player grabs hold of the same spread-open handkerchief with one hand. A player chosen to be the leader stands aside and calls out either "hold fast" or "let go", in which all players must do the opposite. If the leader calls out "hold fast", players must let go of the handkerchief. If "let go" is called out, players must keep hold of it. Those who don't do the opposite of what is called are eliminated.

If more than four players are involved in the game, it is suggested something larger than a handkerchief be used, such as a towel or tablecloth.

Sardines

Sardines is a game much like Hide and Seek, but with a twist. Rather than one person giving all other players time to hide before attempting to find them, Sardines involves just one player hiding while all the others give him/her time to hide before attempting to find that individual.

When one of the seekers finds the player hiding, they then must join that person in hiding in the same location, this action to be repeated by any additional seeker who finds the hiders. Those hiding must remain quiet in order to avoid quick detection.

For example, the game begins and the person selected to be the hider chooses to hide in a crawlspace beneath a stairwell. One of a number of seekers then successfully finds the hider. Without saying anything, that seeker now has to join the hider in that crawlspace. Another seeker may find the two hiders and now must also join those two in the crawlspace. The same goes for the next to find the hiders, the next after that and so on. It can get very cramped all hiding in the same spot, hence the name of this game. The last player to find the hiding space loses the game and is therefore the first person to hide in the next game.

Scissors

Prior to the game beginning, the game host/hostess strings a line across the room on which six threads are hung from. A paper bag containing a prize is attached to each of the six hanging threads. At the start of the game, all players are to get in line. The host/hostess blindfolds the first player and then leads that player to a starting point at which time that player is handed a pair of small scissors. The blindfolded player then takes one step forward and snips with the scissors where he/she believes a paper bag is hanging. The object of the game is for the blindfolded player to cut all six paper bags down, only taking one step between each snip of the scissors and only snipping once at each of the six stops where he/she believes a paper bag is hanging. After snipping six times, that player's turn is over. If they are successful in cutting down any bags, they keep that prize. It is then the next player's turn to repeat the previous player's actions. The game ends when all bags are eventually cut down.

Spirit of the Contrary

One player is chosen to be the game leader, who calls out actions which the other players must do the opposite of. If, for example, the leader says stand up, players must sit down. If the leader says turn to the left, players must turn to the right. If players are told to jump, they must stand still. Any player who doesn't do the opposite of what is called and actually follows the instruction is eliminated. The faster the leader calls out actions, the less time players have to think of doing the opposite of what is called, leading to quicker eliminations, the last player remaining becoming the winner.

The Simpleton

Players are to get in a large circle, preferably extending out to the walls in order to make the circle as large as possible. A player chosen to be the conductor of the game stands in the center of the room. Each player making up the circle decides on a job to perform such as painting a wall, milking a cow, writing a book, etc. The conductor of the game in the center is to mimic playing a flute, moving his/her fingers as if actually playing one.

When the game begins, all players making up the circle begin going through the motions of the job they decided upon. The wall painter paints the wall, the cow milker milks a cow, the writer writes a book, and so on around the circle. Meanwhile, the conductor in the center of the room is pretending to play the flute. At any time, the conductor may switch from playing the flute to copying any job performed by the other players. That player would have to immediately stop what they're doing and take up the conductor's role of playing the flute until the conductor either goes back to playing the flute or switches to another player's job at which point that player immediately switches from playing the flute back to performing their original job.

For example, the conductor quickly changes from playing the flute to going through the motions of painting the wall. The player who is painting the wall has to immediately switch to playing the flute for as long as the conductor is painting the wall. When the conductor either takes up the flute again or changes to another player's job, the wall painter, who was just playing the flute, must immediately return to painting the wall. Any hesitation in switching from job to flute and back again results in that player's elimination from the game. This game requires attention to be paid to the conductor of the game at all times as the conductor may switch to any job at any moment for any length of time.

Early versions of this game, which date back to the 1700s, have the conductor singing the following lyrics while pretending to play the flute:

"When Margaret goes alone,
She does not love me;
The little foolish thing
Is laughing at what I sing;
All I do is no use to me,
Relututu, relututu, relututu"

To add a twist and make this game more challenging, a conversation may be had between all players. A lively conversation may likely lead to distractions in which players will not notice the conductor copying their job, thereby resulting in quicker eliminations.

Snap-Dragon

Snap-Dragon was a game particularly played on Halloween and Christmas Eve and though it has been around for centuries (Shakespeare mentions it in several of his plays), it didn't reach the peak of its popularity until the mid-19th century.

A bowl is filled with brandy. Raisins are then put in the bowl, which will float on the brandy. The brandy is then lit on fire and the lights are turned out, allowing the fire to provide the only lighting in the room. Each player takes a turn sticking their hand into the flaming bowl of brandy in order to retrieve a raisin and eat it as quickly as possible at the risk of being burnt. Whoever retrieves and eats the most raisins without burning their hand or mouth is the winner.

It is likely a combination of injuries and house fires which led to the interest in this game dying out by the late 19th century. Those attempting to play this game today do so at the risk of injury and property damage.

The Tournament

A ring (the smaller the ring the more challenging this game will be) is suspended by a string in the center of the room either from the ceiling, a light fixture or an upright item with an extended arm or hook, such as a coat rack. The ring should be hanging about four feet off the floor. Each player takes a turn running toward the ring with a lance, attempting to get the lance through the ring. The lance can be made of any item at least three feet in length which will pass easily through the ring. A certain number of successful passes through the ring are to be established prior to the start of the game. The first player to reach the determined number of lance passes through the ring is the winner.

Twirling the Trencher

All players take a seat on the floor, aligning themselves in a circle. The larger the room the better as the circle the players create should be fairly large itself.

One player starts the game by taking a round platter and spinning it on its edge in the center of the circle. As soon as the platter is spun, that player must call out the name of any other player seated, then run back to their place in the circle while the player whose name is called jumps up and runs to grab the platter before it falls over. Every spin of the platter will be different. Some spins will last a while and some spins will falter quickly. Either way, the player whose name is called must grab the platter before it falls over to one side. If that player cannot grab the platter before it falls, they are eliminated. If the platter is caught, that player spins it again and calls the name of another, who will then need to repeat the previous actions of running to grab the platter before it falls. The game continues in this manner until there is one player remaining who has not allowed the platter to fall over, thus becoming the winner.

Where Is Your Letter Going?

Chairs are arranged around the edges of the room to make for as much space in the center of the room as possible. One player is chosen to be the postmaster and another is chosen to be the carrier. All other players are to take a seat in the chairs. Each seated player is given the name of a town or city anywhere in the world by the postmaster, in which that player now represents that location. It helps if the postmaster writes down which location is associated with each player so as to not forgot any locations. The carrier is blindfolded and stands in the center of the room while the postmaster stands off to the side, out of the area of play. The carrier cannot remove the blindfold for the duration of the game. The postmaster then says, for example, "I have a letter to go from Philadelphia to Los Angeles" or "I have a letter to go from Dallas to Paris". The players representing those cities must then jump up and quickly swap seats. In doing so, the blindfolded carrier attempts to grab one of the players, in which those players must avoid capture. If the carrier is successful in grabbing a player, he/she must guess who they have a hold of. If guessed correctly, the player captured becomes the carrier. If guessed incorrectly, the current blindfolded player remains the carrier. If the postmaster says "I have letters to go all over the world", all players must jump up and change seats in which the blindfolded carrier then tries to claim one of the seats for him/herself. If the carrier is successful in obtaining a seat, the player remaining without a seat now becomes the carrier. Caution should be taken while playing this game as it could be dangerous, especially for the carrier, who will be running while blindfolded.

The Wolf and the Dog

This game consisted of one gentleman and all other players being ladies. The gentleman is the wolf. The oldest lady is designated the dog. All the other ladies line up behind the dog, making up the dog's tail, collectively. The object for the wolf is to try to capture the final segment of the dog's tail, which would be the last lady in line.

The wolf (the gentleman) and the dog (the first lady in line) start off the game facing each other. The wolf, in an attempt to capture the last segment of the dog's tail (the last lady in line), will need to get around the first lady, who extends her arms and moves along with him in an attempt to block him from getting past her to the end of the tail. If the wolf gets past the first lady in line attempting to block him, the last lady in line, making up the end of the dog's tail, must immediately run to the front of the line and place herself in front of the first lady before being captured by the wolf. The wolf may not break through the line of ladies (the tail) to capture the one running. He must only run on either side of the tail. If successful in reaching the front of the line before being captured, that lady remains at the front as the new dog and now becomes the one attempting to block the wolf from again getting to the end of the tail and capturing the lady now making up the last segment of the tail. If, however, the wolf gets past the first lady in line trying to block him and successfully captures the last lady in line trying to get to the front, she is eliminated but not before she receives her punishment of being kissed by the wolf. If enough ladies are successful in making it from the end of the tail to the front so that the original oldest lady starting off as the dog now finds herself as the last segment of the tail, the wolf loses and the game is over. If the wolf manages to capture all the ladies, leaving only the oldest one remaining before she can become the last segment of the tail, the wolf wins the game.

If You Love Me Dearest, Smile

All players sit around a table. One player is chosen to be "it". That player must get every other player around the table, one by one, to smile using facial expressions and gestures. Eye contact must be kept with each player at all times. Talking is not permitted by any players. A time limit may be set in the attempt at getting each player to smile. If a player smiles, they are eliminated from the game. If one cannot be made to smile and time runs out, the player who is "it" must move on to the next player and keep going around the table until only one player remains who has not been made to smile, thus becoming the winner. The winner, or any other player agreed upon, then becomes "it" and the game starts over in the same manner.

Additionally, any player at the table not currently being challenged by "it" may relax and even smile if they wish. It is only when challenged by "it" that one may not smile. Players, however, cannot attempt to help "it" get another player to smile or that player will eliminate themselves from the game.

At a time when keeping long eye contact with someone of the opposite gender with whom you were not in a relationship with was considered inappropriate, the game of "If You Love Me Dearest, Smile" was popular among adults in the 19th century, as it voided this unwritten rule. This game allowed ladies and gentlemen to keep eye contact with each other for long periods of time and to flirt openly in this manner. This simple game is said to have likely led to many new relationships.

Laughing Game

All players are to form a circle. Each player takes a turn, in order, saying either "Ha", "Ho" or "Hee". These must be said quickly, resulting in possible mispronunciations such as "Hey" instead of "Hee", "Haw" instead of "Ha", etc. Pronunciation is important. If a player mispronounces "Ha", "Ho" or "Hee", they are eliminated. Any player who laughs during the game is also eliminated. The player remaining who has not mispronounced any words or laughed is the winner.

Laughter

Players sit in a circle where they must be silent. One player throws a handkerchief into the air. Immediately, all players begin laughing but must immediately stop upon the handkerchief hitting the ground. If any player continues laughing for even a moment upon the handkerchief hitting the ground, they are eliminated. The last player remaining is the winner, though that player may continue playing the game by him/herself, to the amusement of the others, if they wish.

Pinch Without Laughing

Players sit side by side or in a circle taking turns pinching their neighbor's nose. The object of the game is to be the player who laughs the least amount of times within a certain number of laughs allowed, determined prior to beginning the game. For instance, if two laughs are determined to be the maximum amount of times a player may laugh, any player who laughs a third time is eliminated from the game, the player remaining who has not yet laughed three times becoming the winner. No other method of getting players to laugh is allowed other than pinching a neighbor's nose. It doesn't necessarily have to be the neighbor whose nose is getting pinched who laughs. If anyone in the game laughs, that's a strike against them. A player may pinch a neighbor's nose as lightly or as hard as they choose.

At the height of this game's popularity in the 1850s, players resorted to trickery in order to get others to laugh. Players would sometimes blacken their index finger and thumb with burnt cork, leaving black smudges on a person's nose, causing others in the game to laugh.

Poor Pussy

Players form a large circle around the room, with the exception of one who is chosen to be the cat, known as Pussy. Pussy crawls on all fours toward any other player he/she wishes, then kneels in front of that player and meows. The player who Pussy is kneeling in front of must pet him/her while sympathetically saying "Poor Pussy, Poor Pussy, Poor Pussy" without smiling or laughing. Pussy may meow in any way he/she wishes and may also make faces in an attempt to get the person petting him/her to smile or laugh. If that person smiles or laughs before getting through sympathetically saying "Poor Pussy, Poor Pussy, Poor Pussy", that player becomes Pussy and gameplay continues on. Variations of this game have the person playing Pussy blindfolded so as to add more humor to the game with a player blindly crawling around, possibly into a wall. There are no eliminations in this game. It continues on for as long as players wish.

The Sculptor

One player is selected to be the sculptor. All other players must stand in place motionless. The sculptor goes around to each motionless player and one by one, positions them in poses which are difficult to hold. The other players must not laugh, break pose or move. While sculpting one player, the sculptor may attempt to distract other players, encouraging them to either move or laugh but must not touch any player other than the one he/she is sculpting. The first player to laugh, break pose or move loses and becomes the sculptor in the next game. The following image depicts a forfeit, as mentioned in the Foreword, in which someone who would have been eliminated from a game instead pays a forfeit (punishment), in this case allowing themselves to be positioned in strange poses. Though a forfeit, this is still a fair depiction of how The Sculptor is played.

Throwing the Smile

Players sit in a circle in which only one player is allowed to smile. All other players must appear neutral. The player smiling may attempt to get other players to smile by using facial expressions and actions, though words cannot be used. If successful in making other players smile, those players are eliminated. When the player smiling is ready, he/she then wipes their hand over their smile as if to grab and remove it from their face in which they must immediately appear neutral. They then throw the smile to any other player in the circle, who catches it, wiping it onto their own face. That player may then smile until they too remove the smile from their face, immediately becoming neutral and throwing the smile to someone else. These actions continue throughout the game, with the only person smiling being the one who catches the smile and only after wiping it onto their face. Whoever is currently in possession of the smile may keep it and smile for as long as they wish. The only time a player is eliminated from the game after catching the thrown smile is if he/she smiles prior to wiping it onto their face or continues smiling momentarily after wiping it off.

A unique insight
into the obscure
history of
America's 19th
and early 20th
century

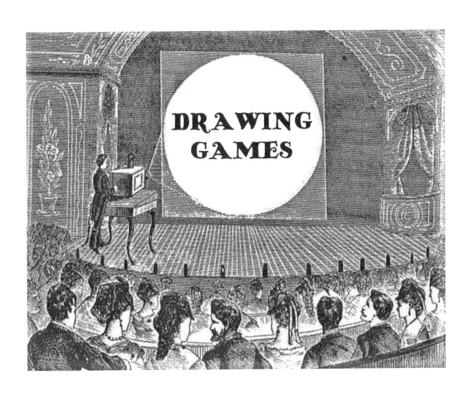

The Artist's Menagerie

Players sit around a table. Each player is provided a sheet of paper and a pencil. At the top of the paper, each player draws a head. It could be the head of a human, animal, bird, fish, whatever the player chooses. Once everyone has drawn a head, the portion of the paper in which the head appears must be folded back and out of sight, exactly at where the drawing at the base of the head ends. All papers are then passed to the player on the left. The players now receiving the sheet of paper then draw a neck and torso, including arms if necessary, beginning at the very top of the paper where it is folded back. The torso, like the head, could be of a human, animal, etc. The players must not unfold the paper or look at the back of it in order to see the head. Upon finishing drawing the neck, torso and/or arms, that portion of the paper is then folded back and out of sight at exactly where the drawing ends. The papers are then passed again to the players on the left, who draw the bottom half of the body, again beginning at the very top of the paper where it is folded back. The drawings now complete, the papers are passed once more to the left, in which, one by one, they are unfolded so everyone can see all three parts of the body drawn together as one. The only objective of this game is to enjoy the mishmash of characters created by players who were not aware of what the previous player had drawn.

The Drawing Game

Players (artists) sit around a table, each one provided with a sheet of paper and a pencil. Each artist makes a very rough sketch at the top of their paper, illustrating some well-known scene from an event associated with history, entertainment, etc. When all artists are finished drawing, they each pass their sketch to their neighbor on the left, who looks at the sketch and writes at the bottom of the paper what they think it represents, along with their name. The sketches keep getting passed to the left until everyone has had a chance to write their guess on what they think each sketch portrays. When everyone has finished writing their guesses and names and the sketches make their way back to the artists who drew them, each artist then takes turns saying what they drew and then reads off all the guesses. Those who correctly guessed what was sketched earn a point, hence the names next to the guesses being necessary. There are no eliminations in this game. All players remain involved in the game for as many rounds the players wish the game to last, at which time the player with the most points awarded (who has made the most correct guesses) is the winner.

Portrait

For this game, there need to be an equal number of ladies and gentlemen. All players are seated at a rectangular table, ladies sitting on one side and gentlemen sitting opposite them on the other. The game host/hostess provides each player with a sheet of paper and pencil. Each gentleman will need to draw the lady's face sitting across from him and the lady will need to draw the gentleman's face across from her. At the host/hostess's signal, the players are given five minutes to complete this task. The players should keep in mind that only the face is to be drawn. Hair, earrings or any other features on the head are to be avoided so as not to make a drawing easily identifiable. If a person has identifying features on their face such as facial hair, moles, beauty marks or freckles, they are to be omitted from the drawings so as to also not make a drawing easily identifiable. The main focus should be the eyes, nose and mouth. When five minutes are up, the gentlemen move over a seat so they are now sitting across from a different lady. Each player is again given a sheet of paper and five minutes to draw the face of the new person across from them. Gameplay continues in this manner until all ladies and gentlemen have had a chance to draw each other's face. The host/hostess then collects all the drawings, numbers them and pins or tapes them up on a wall for all to see. Each player is then provided another sheet of paper in which they are to write the number of each drawing and the name of who they believe the drawing is of. The person who correctly identifies the most faces wins a prize. A prize is also awarded to the best artist.

Retsch's Outlines
or Outlines

All players sit at a table and are provided a sheet of paper and a pencil. Each player draws a single line. The line could be straight, curved, squiggled or any shape the player desires. Pressure must be applied to make the line dark. All sheets are then passed to the player on the left who must make a drawing from the line already on the paper. The amount of time allowed for this is typically five minutes. The drawing could be as simple or as detailed as a player wishes to make it. The original line drawn, however, must remain darker than the drawing itself so when shown to everyone else, they can see the original line worked with to make that drawing. There are no points awarded or eliminations. The only objective of this game is to enjoy how creative players can be with just a single line provided to them.

Though the last name differs in spelling, this game is named after Friedrich August Moritz Retzsh, an early 19th century German painter, better known for his black and white etchings of scenes from books and plays.

Sight Unseen

A player is selected as the game host/hostess. The other players are divided into multiple teams of two so that everyone has a partner. If there is an uneven number of players, the host/hostess may participate in the game. Each team is provided with a sheet of paper and a pencil and decide amongst themselves which one is the best artist, in which he/she will be the one to draw. The other is given a common object to describe to his/her partner. All teams are seated at a table but those partnered must be facing away from each other so the person drawing cannot see the object their partner is holding. At the host/hostess's signal to begin, the person holding the object describes it to their partner who draws it. The more descriptive one can be with the item they're holding, the more detailed their partner can make the drawing. After a certain amount of time determined prior to the start of the game, the host/hostess collects the drawings and objects and places them side by side for all to see. All then decide by vote which drawing best resembles the object it represents, in which those partners are the winning team.

Zoological Competition

Prior to the start of the game, the host/hostess is to cut up many strips of paper, writing the name of an animal on each one. The strips of paper are than all put into a bowl or box.

When the game begins, each player is provided a sheet of paper and scissors. Each player then pulls out a strip of paper with an animal's name on it from the bowl or box. Players must not tell anyone what animal they have selected. Once all players have pulled the name of an animal, they then have ten minutes to cut out the shape of that animal from the sheet of paper. Players are not allowed to draw the animal beforehand. Once ten minutes are up, the host/

hostess collects all the cutouts, numbers each one and pins or tapes them to a wall for all to see. The host/hostess then provides a slip of paper to each player, in which each player votes on the best cutout (the cutout in which they can best decipher what the animal is supposed to be) and the worst (the cutout in which it is the toughest to decipher what the animal is supposed to be). The player responsible for the cutout receiving the greatest number of "best" votes wins a prize and the one receiving the greatest number of "worst" votes wins a booby prize. When the game is finished, players may then tell everyone what their animal cutouts are supposed to be.

MEMORY &
GUESSING
GAMES

Advice

Players sit around a table, each one provided with a slip of paper and a pencil. Each player writes a piece of advice, whether good or bad, then folds the paper and passes it to his/her neighbor on the right. One by one, before the neighbors unfold the slip of paper to read the advice, they must guess beforehand whether the advice is good or bad. The players who make a correct guess prior to unfolding the paper receive a point. For instance, if a player says he/she believes the advice is good and then unfolds the paper to read "Look both ways before crossing a street", that is good advice and that player who guessed correctly receives a point. However, if a player says the advice is good and then unfolds the paper to read "It is safe to walk on railroad tracks", that is bad advice and because the player guessed incorrectly, receives no point. If, however, that player had said the advice was bad before unfolding the paper, they would be correct and receive a point. The player who first reaches the amount of points necessary to win the game, as is determined prior to starting it, is the winner.

The Adjective Game

One player is chosen to be the guesser and leaves the room. The other players choose an adjective which the guesser will have to identify. Once called back into the room, the guesser asks each person a question regarding anything they wish; it doesn't necessarily have to be related to the game. Each person must answer the question in the manner of the adjective selected.

For example, if players select the adjective, "angry", the guesser can ask a player a question such as "What did you have for lunch today?" in which that player would have to answer in an angry manner. The guesser may then ask another player, "What is your favorite breed of dog?", in which that player would also have to answer in an angry manner. Whichever player's answer allows the guesser to correctly identify the adjective, that player then becomes the guesser and the game begins anew.

Alphabetical Character Guessing

For the description of this game, I will identify players with numbers as this can otherwise become a bit tricky to follow. One player is selected to be the guesser and leaves the room while the others select the name of a character from a book (or movie/television show if pulling characters from more modern forms of entertainment). The character selected should be fairly known by most people. The character selected for this example is Charlie Chaplin. However, the name Chaplin will be played as only last names of characters are allowed. Each player would then be assigned a letter from "Chaplin" in which they then must think of a name beginning with that letter, whether it be someone fictional or real. For example, Player 1 will be assigned the letter "C" and may think of Cleopatra, which begins with that letter. Player 2 will then be assigned the letter "H" and may think of the cartoon character He-Man. Player 3 will then be assigned the letter "A" and may think of Aphrodite, the Greek goddess of love. Player 4 will then be assigned the letter "P" and may think of Poe (Edgar Allen). This continues on down the line until each player is assigned a letter in the character's name and thinks of someone whose name begins with that letter.

The guesser is then called back into the room, where he/she must identify the original character (Chaplin) based on the names each player thought of in connection with their letter.

Starting from the player who represents the first letter, the guesser attempts to identify the name thought of which will ultimately lead to the letter assigned to that player. As each letter is uncovered, the guesser will be able to identify the original character name.

To demonstrate, the guesser will ask Player 1, "Is your character real or fictitious?" Upon receiving the answer, he/she will then ask, "Is your character historical, biblical, political, literary, in film, television or music?" Upon receiving the answer, the guesser will continue asking questions of Player 1 until he/she figures out the character is Cleopatra, thereby realizing the first letter of the original character is "C". The guesser will then move on to Player 2, asking the same questions until he/she identifies the character as He-Man, thereby knowing the second letter of the original character is "H". This continues on down the line until the guesser has accumulated enough letters of the original character to know who it is. The guesser may, at any point, state who he/she believes the original character is, based on the letters uncovered. If the guess is incorrect, the guesser continues on down the line asking questions until more letters have been revealed of the original character. When the guesser correctly identifies who the original character is, in this case Chaplin, the player whose assigned letter allowed the guesser to correctly identify the original character becomes the guesser in the next game.

The Cook Who Does Not Like Peas

One player is designated the leader of this food-themed game and chooses a letter without telling the others what it is, in which that letter is the secret letter to be guessed by the others. In order to correctly guess what the secret letter is, foods containing that letter are dismissed. This game requires strong attention and memory.

Though this game is titled "The Cook Who Does Not Like Peas", which is a play on the letter P, any letter may take the place of P. To demonstrate, the leader of the game selects the secret letter T and then says to the other players, "My cook does not like tomatoes; what shall we give him/her to eat?" Notice "tomatoes" contains the letter T, hence why it's chosen to start the game as a food the cook does not like. One by one, players name two foods. Perhaps the first player may say, "chicken and carrots". Because carrots contain the letter T, the leader then says, "He/She does not like them" and moves on to the next player. Even though "chicken" does not contain the letter T, it is still included in foods the cook does not like because it accompanied "carrots". Perhaps the next player then says, "apples and pizza". Because neither word contains the letter T, the leader would say, "Yes, he/she likes them" and then moves on again to the next player.

Players need to remember which foods the cook does not like and then find a pattern among the disliked foods, eventually realizing that of all the pairs of foods the cook does not like, one food in each pair contained the letter T and therefore that must be the secret letter. The same foods may be named multiple times during the game by any player. Using the example above, chicken was a food the cook did not like the first time it was mentioned because it accompanied carrots, which contained the letter T. However, if another player happens to say chicken and bread, then chicken would be a food the cook does in fact like this time around since it accompanies bread, which does not contain a T. Therefore players, if paying attention, will recognize that chicken and bread, as well as apples and pizza mentioned above, do not contain the secret letter but that chicken was not liked when it accompanied carrots. Also, the game started with the cook not liking tomatoes. If a player thinks he/she knows the secret letter, they must wait their turn before guessing what that secret letter is. Their guess of the letter will take place of their food guess, meaning if it is their turn, instead of saying two foods, they may guess what the secret letter is. Players cannot name foods and guess the secret letter during the same turn. If the secret letter guessed is incorrect, the leader moves on to the next player, who also may either say two more foods or take a guess at the secret letter if he/she believes they know what that letter is. The first player to correctly identify the secret letter wins the game and becomes the leader in the next game.

This game can be challenging due to the amount of memorization required. Until players grasp the game well, they may want to write down the pairs of foods the cook does not like, thereby being able to see letter patterns.

Dumb Crambo
or Acting Rhymes

Players are divided into two teams. The teams decide which is to be the guessing team. We'll call the guessing team Team B and the other Team A. Each team goes into a separate room where they cannot see or hear the other. Team A must think of a word containing one syllable. For example, the word chosen is "cook".

A player from team A goes to notify Team B that a word has been selected and rhymes with "hook". All players on Team B discuss amongst themselves and come to a decision on what they believe the word is. They then enter the room Team A is in and act out the word. For instance, if Team B thinks the word is "book", all players must act out reading or writing a book. Since that is the incorrect word, players on Team A then hiss at Team B in which Team B goes back to their original room to discuss another word. Perhaps Team B now believes the word is "took". They all come back into Team A's room and pretend to take things from one another. Again being the wrong word, Team B again gets hissed and must go back and think of another word. Now believing the word is "cook", Team B comes back into the room and acts out cooking such as stirring a pot or shaking spices into food (players may act out different actions as long as it relates to the word agreed upon by Team B). This being the correct word guessed, Team A claps for Team B. The two teams then swap roles for the next game, Team A now being the guessing team. No verbal communication by either team is to occur when both teams are together, other than one team hissing at another team's incorrect guess. Also, no clues may be provided. There are no points awarded or eliminations. The game continues on for as long as players wish.

Eyes

A sheet is hung in the center of the room in which two holes for eyes are cut out. Players are divided into two teams, one team standing on one side of the sheet and the other team standing on the other side. One by one, a player from each team walks up to the sheet and peers through the eyeholes into the eyes of the player on the other side. Each player must identify who that other player is based on just their eyes. If correct, that team receives a point. The next player from each team then approaches the sheet, making the same guess as to whose eyes they are looking into. Then the next players approach the sheet and so on down the line. In order to not have the same pair of eyes peering through the eyeholes at a certain turn within a rotation, teams may change rotation to keep the other team guessing. The team which reaches a certain number of points first, established at the start of the game, wins.

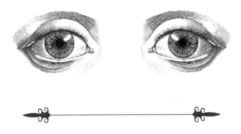

Fictionary

Players form a circle. A dictionary is passed around among all players and one by one, each selects a word from it which is not well known. Each player then writes that word on a sheet of paper along with the real definition and two made up definitions. When all players have written their word and definitions, Player 1 then reads aloud his/her selected word from the dictionary and the three definitions, one of which is the real definition of the word. Going around the circle, each player says what they believe the correct definition of the word is. Player 1 tells everyone what the correct definition is only after all players have taken a guess. For every incorrect guess made, Player 1 receives a point. It is then Player 2's turn to read his/her selected word and definitions, again receiving a point for every incorrect definition guessed by the others, and so on around the circle until all players have had a turn reading their selected word and definitions and all definition guesses have been made. At this point, the game may either end or additional rounds may be played, in which all players must select a new word from the dictionary and come up with two more made up definitions to accompany the real one. Once it is decided the game is to end, whichever player has the most points (that is, who has fooled the most players into guessing a word's definition incorrectly) is the winner.

The Game of Cat

One player is chosen to be "it" who leaves the room, going into another and shutting the door. One by one, all other players come to the closed door and say "meow" through it in a disguised voice. On the other side of the closed door, "it" must identify which player said "meow". If guessed correctly, the first player who was identified becomes "it" and the game continues on for as long as players wish.

The Game of Location

Players are divided into two teams. In this example, we'll call them Team A and Team B. A map of the world is laid on the ground or table or a globe is brought into the room. Player 1 from Team A says the name of a location from anywhere in the world in which

Player 1 from Team B has to locate, placing their finger on that location on the map or globe within the count of 20, to be counted aloud by Player 1 on Team A. Other players must not assist their teammate in finding locations. If Player 1 on Team B finds and places his/her finger on the location on the map or globe within the count of 20, no changes are made to either team. However, if Player 1 from Team B is unsuccessful in finding the location within the count of 20, Team A then steals a player of their choosing from Team B. The roles of the teams are then reversed, with Player 2 from Team B saying the name of a location in which Player 2 from Team A must locate before the count of 20, which Player 2 from Team B counts aloud. Again, if a location is identified within the count of 20, no changes are made but if the location cannot be identified within the count of 20, Team B then steals a player of their choosing from Team A. Player 3 from Team A then challenges Player 3 from Team B in the same manner, the gameplay continuing back and forth this way until one team has obtained all players from the other. When one team is down to their last player and that player is unable to successfully find a location on the map or globe before the count of 20, it thereby ends the game.

Hiss and Clap

Only ladies may speak during this game. Gentlemen are to remain silent. All gentlemen are requested to leave the room while the ladies take a seat on a chair, sofa, bench, etc with a vacant seat next to each lady. The ladies choose amongst themselves who they want their gentleman partner to be, in which that gentleman, upon re-entering the room, must take a seat next to the lady he believes has chosen him for her partner. One by one, the gentlemen are called into the room by the ladies and asked which one he thinks has chosen him for her partner. The ladies, if they wish, may attempt to trick each gentleman into guessing incorrectly by flirting with him. Without saying anything, the gentleman must then sit in a vacant seat next to the lady he believes has chosen him. If he chooses correctly, the ladies applaud. The gentleman then stands from the seat and off to the side, remaining in the room with the ladies. All gentlemen who make a correct guess may remain in the room. The next gentleman is then called in and goes through the same routine. If he sits in a vacant seat next to a lady who has not chosen him for her partner, the ladies hiss and that gentleman must leave the room, re-joining the others, to make a second successful guess when it's his turn again to come back in. The game ends when all gentlemen have successfully chosen the vacant seat next to the lady who selected him for her partner.

How? Why? When? Where?

One player is selected to be the thinker, who must think of an object. The other players, in a chosen order, must try to guess what object the thinker is thinking of by asking the following four questions. Each question can be asked only once.

Player 2: "How do you like it?"
Player 3: "Why do you like it?"
Player 4: "When do you like it?"
Player 5: "Where do you like it?"

With the thinker having answered the four questions, the other players quickly attempt to guess what the object is as the example below demonstrates.

Player 2: "How do you like it?"
Thinker: "On."
Player 3: "Why do you like it?"
Thinker: "It creates memories."
Player 4: "When do you like it?"
Thinker: "When I'm on vacation."
Player 5: "Where do you like it?"
Thinker: "In my hands."

Some or all of the players may then correctly be thinking the object is a camera. The first to shout out what the object is wins. That player then becomes the thinker in the next game. If no one guesses the object correctly, the current thinker then starts a new game, choosing another object to think of.

I'm Thinking of Something

A player is selected to be the thinker, who must think of something, whether it be a person, place, object, etc. The thinker then must give hints to the other players as to what he/she is thinking. If, for example, the thinker is thinking of a hummingbird, he/she would say, "I'm thinking of something small". Obviously not enough information for other players to make a guess as to what it is, the thinker may follow it up by saying, "I'm thinking of something that flies". There is only one chance among all players combined to correctly guess what the thinker is thinking of. If a player guesses correctly, that player becomes the thinker and the game starts anew. If an incorrect guess is given, that game ends and the person who is currently the thinker must think of something else, as they'll remain the thinker in the next game.

Kim's Game

Named after Rudeyard Kipling's 1901 novel, "Kim", a player is selected to be the presenter. The presenter places a number of small items on a tray, all of which are unrelated. Players are given a slip of paper and pencil and two minutes to examine the tray and try to memorize the items on it. The tray is then covered up and all players must make a list of as many items they can remember. The player who memorizes the most items on the tray is the winner and becomes the presenter for the next game, placing new items on the tray.

The Little Old Man's House

All players form a circle. One player starts the game by saying, "I sell you my little old man's house." The next player in the circle then adds their own item to sell which is related to the previous item but also must repeat what the previous player said. The game continues going around the circle as each player adds a new item to sell while also repeating every previous item sold in the correct order as per the example below.

Player 1: "I sell you my little old man's house."
Player 2: "I sell you the door of my little old man's house."
Player 3: "I sell you the lock to the door of my little old man's house."
Player 4: "I sell you the key for the lock to the door of my little old man's house."
Player 5: "I sell you the bird that grabbed the key for the lock to the door of my little old man's house."
Player 6: "I sell you the cat that caught the bird that grabbed the key to the lock of the door of my little old man's house."
Etc, etc...

Though this game is called "The Little Old Man's House", any object may take the place of the house to begin the game.

If, during their turn, a player fails to repeat any previous item sold in the correct order, that player is eliminated. The player remaining who can repeat every previous item sold in the correct order, or as much of the correct order as possible, is the winner.

Living Pictures

The more players involved, the more creative this game can become. Players are divided into two teams. One team (the guessing team) leaves the room while the other team (the posing team) decides on a well-known scene to re-create. The scene could be one from an historical event, a painting, a book or for a more modern take, a scene from a movie or television show (Shakespearean scenes were popular in this game during the 19th century). When the posing team has decided on a scene to re-create, they get into the appropriate poses and remain still, as if frozen in a picture, hence the name of the game. They then call the guessing team back into the room.

Upon the guessing team entering the room and seeing the posing team frozen in a scene, they then have to guess what scene is being portrayed. No verbal communication may occur by the posing team while the guessing team is trying to identify the scene. There are no eliminations in this game. The game ends when the guessing team either correctly identifies the scene being portrayed or when they give up, unable to correctly identify it. In either case, the two teams then swap roles and a new game begins.

Lookabout

A player is selected to be the host/hostess. The host/hostess selects a small item in the room, a thimble for example, then picks it up and shows it to the other players. The other players must now leave the room while the host/hostess "hides" the item in plain sight in a different location within that room. The item should be hidden just enough that it's visible but may take a bit of searching to locate it due to it being small, especially if placed among other small items. Upon the host/hostess calling the others to re-enter the room, the players walk in and start looking around for that item. When a player spots the item, they must not say anything but instead quietly take a seat. The last player standing looking for the item loses the game and becomes the host/hostess for the next game, now becoming the one who must hide an item.

Magic Music

This game is an earlier version of the popular game Hot and Cold and requires at least one person who can play a piano, though other instruments may be substituted.

A player is chosen to be the finder, who is told what item is going to be hidden in the room. The finder then leaves the room while the other players hide that item. When the finder is called back in, he/she must look for the hidden item. The player at the piano begins playing a tune once the search for that item begins, playing louder when the finder gets closer to the hidden item and softer when the finder is moving away from it. The finder will eventually be able to locate the hidden item, being guided only by the sound of the music. When the finder locates the item, the music is to stop, signifying the hidden item has been found.

The Mimic Club

All players except two leave the room. The two players remaining are club members and sit side by side in chairs with a single chair in front of them, facing them. The players who left the room are club applicants. The club members must decide on a name for their club, which can either be serious or absurd. Either way, it should be a name which can be acted out either with or without verbal clues. The members decide which one of the two is going to act out the name of the club and which one is going to mimic that member's movements and/or verbal clues. For example, the club name the two members choose is Crunchy Frisbee. The first club applicant is called into the room and takes a seat in the chair facing the two members. One of the members begins making mouth movements and/or crunching sounds, providing clues to the first word "Crunchy" in which the other member must mimic simultaneously. Then the word "Frisbee" is acted out. One club member may act out throwing and catching a frisbee, in which the other club member must again mimic simultaneously. The applicant must guess the name of the club based on both members' simultaneous movements and/or verbal clues. There are no eliminations in this game. Applicants continue to guess the name of the club until they guess correctly. They then become a member of the club, pull up a chair next to the other two members and the next applicant is called in to take a seat in front of the now three club members. The newest member of the club now must act out, with or without verbal clues, the name of the club, Crunchy Frisbee, and the two original club members must mimic everything the newest member does and says. When the applicant correctly guesses the name of the club, he/she then pulls up a chair next to the other members, now being the one to provide the clues to the next applicant, in which the other members must mimic simultaneously. Each time a new member joins the club, that member becomes the one who decides on the actions and words which the other previous members must mimic. Since all members must mimic the newest club member, including being seated, there should be enough chairs for all players.

Nuts to Crack

Each player is provided a pencil and sheet of paper with the following clues already written on it by the game leader.

1. A dairy product
2. A vegetable
3. A country
4. A girl's name
5. A structure
6. A name often applied to one of our presidents
7. Every ocean has one

8. That which often holds a treasure
9. The names of two boys
10. A letter of the alphabet and an article made of tin

The game leader then explains that the names of ten types of nuts can be obtained by the clues provided on the paper. Whichever player guesses and writes down the most correct names of nuts based on the clues provided is the winner (the winner was often awarded a small prize).

There is only one correct type of nut associated with each clue, which are as follows:

1. Butternut
2. Peanut
3. Brazil nut
4. Hazelnut
5. Walnut
6. Hickory nut (Seventh President Andrew Jackson was known as Old Hickory, a nickname he received for being a strict and bold military officer during the War of 1812)
7. Beechnut
8. Chestnut
9. Filbert (Phil and Bert)
10. Pecan

Pass the Slipper

Players form a circle, either seated or standing. Another player, chosen to be a guesser, stands in the center of that circle. The guesser closes their eyes and while they're closed, the players making up the circle pass a slipper (or other small object) behind their backs along to one another. When the guesser opens their eyes at any moment they choose, the passing of the slipper or small object is to immediately stop and the guesser has to identify who is currently holding the slipper/object. All players making up the circle must keep their hands behind their back the entire game so as to try and trick the guesser as to who is actually holding the slipper/object at any given moment. If the guesser correctly identifies the person holding the slipper/object, that person then becomes the guesser in the next game. If guessed incorrectly, the player currently in the center of the circle remains the guesser.

Pointer's Buff

Players stand in a circle while the player selected to be the guesser stands in the center. The guesser is blindfolded and holds a stick (a rod, pencil, candle, etc may be used in place of a stick if desired). The players making up the circle either walk, run, skip, etc. around the guesser. At any moment, the guesser holds out the stick at which point all those in the circle stop moving. Whichever person in the circle finds him/herself in front of the outstretched stick must grab a hold of it. The guesser must then identify who is holding the stick by asking any question in which the player holding the stick must try to trick the guesser by answering in a disguised voice. If the guesser incorrectly identifies who is holding the stick, the game starts over without any player changes. If the guesser is correct in identifying someone through their disguised voice, that individual identified becomes the guesser in the next game.

Scents

Prior to the start of this game, the host/hostess will have already lined up a row of bottles on a table. The bottles should be dark so as not to see the contents inside. A different liquid is poured into each one. Not much liquid is needed, though the scent should be noticeable enough that players won't have to inhale too deeply in order to smell the contents inside. The fluids may consist of beverages, cleaning solutions, medicines, etc. The bottles are numbered and slips of paper for each player are numbered to correspond with each bottle.

At the start of the game, players enter the room in which the bottles are set up. The host/hostess hands each player a pencil and as many slips of paper as there are bottles, each slip of paper already containing a number on it to correspond with each numbered bottle. One by one, players approach the first bottle, smelling its contents and writing down what they believe the contents are, along with their name, on that corresponding paper. They then turn the slip of paper over, leaving it next to that bottle and move on to the second bottle, doing the same thing for that one, then moving on to the third, fourth, etc. Once all players have had a chance to guess what they believe the contents of each bottle are, the host/hostess takes the slips of paper from the first bottle and reads aloud what each player's guess is. Once all guesses are read, the host/hostess then reveals what the liquid actually is. Those who guessed correctly receive a point. The reveal of each bottle's contents continues on down the line and when done, the player with the most points wins. If there is a tie, those players who have tied leave the room and the host/hostess refills the bottles with different liquids for a tie-breaking round. If another tie

occurs, another tie-breaking round is then played and so on until
there is a winner.

Shadow Buff

A white bedsheet is hung on a line stretched across the room.
A candle or lamp is placed on a table on one side of the sheet. A
player selected to be the guesser is positioned on the other side of
the sheet at least 15 feet away from it, though preferably a bit farther
if there is enough space. The lights are then turned off, though the
candle or lamp is to remain lit. One by one, players walk behind the
bedsheet, in between the sheet and candle/lamp. The light from the
candle/lamp will throw the player's shadow onto the bedsheet and
the guesser on the other side has to guess which player it is based on
that shadow. Players may attempt to disguise their shadow in any
way, such as changing the way they walk, wearing accessories, etc.
in order to trick the guesser into guessing incorrectly. If the guesser
correctly identifies a player's shadow, that player whose shadow was
identified becomes the guesser. There are no eliminations in this
game. The game continues on for as long as players wish.

Shouting Proverbs

This game can be rather noisy. One player is chosen to be the guesser and leaves the room while the other players choose a proverb. For instance, the proverb chosen may be "An apple a day keeps the doctor away" or "Beauty is in the eye of the beholder". Using the former as an example, each player is assigned a prominent word from the proverb, in this case "apple", "day", "doctor" and "away". One player may be assigned "apple", another is assigned "day", another is assigned "doctor" and so on. If there are more players than words, some players may be assigned the same word. Once a proverb is selected and each player is assigned their appropriate word from that proverb, the guesser is called back into the room. Once back in the room and at the count of three, each player shouts their assigned word simultaneously. The guesser, based on the words he/she picks out from the simultaneous shouts, must identify what the proverb is. Players may only shout once. It is up to the guesser to identify the proverb after the first simultaneous shout. If the guesser cannot correctly identify the proverb, he/she must leave the room and come back again when the other players have selected another proverb, to be shouted in the same manner as before. If guessed correctly, another player becomes the guesser. There are no points awarded or eliminations. The game lasts for as long as players wish.

Squeak, Piggy, Squeak

A player selected to be the farmer is blindfolded and given a pillow. The farmer remains standing while all other players (the piggies) are seated in a circle closely around him/her. The farmer spins around until disoriented and then drops the pillow. Whichever seated piggy's lap the pillow drops into must squeak/squeal like a pig. The farmer attempts to guess who that player is based only on the sound of their squeak/squeal. If guessed correctly, that player who squeaked/squealed then becomes the farmer. If guessed incorrectly, the pillow is returned to the current farmer and the game starts anew, all actions above being repeated.

A variation of the game involves the farmer placing the pillow on a piggy's lap and then sitting on that pillow on their lap rather than just dropping it. However, due to a number of reasons such as potential injury or just the fact that people don't necessarily want to be sat on, simply dropping the pillow into a player's lap appears to be the more popular version of the game.

The Stool of Repentance

A player is chosen to be the guesser and leaves the room while others write on slips of paper their opinion of the guesser. For instance, one person may write "She has a great sense of humor". Another may write "She is selfish". When all players' opinions of the guesser are written, one of the players is chosen to be the reader of those opinions. The guesser is then called back into the room, where the reader reads the slips of paper aloud. The guesser has to identify which person wrote what about him/her. Only one chance to identify the writer of each opinion is allowed. The first person correctly identified in connection with the written opinion becomes the guesser in the next game. This game can obviously be hurtful to players so rules may want to be established as to omitting negative opinions.

Tea-Pot

One player is chosen to be the guesser and leaves the room. All other players decide on a secret word with multiple meanings which the guesser will have to correctly identify. The guesser is then called back into the room. One at a time, but in no particular order, each player states a sentence to another, substituting the secret word with "Tea-Pot". In the example below, let's assume the secret word is "fly". Upon the guesser being called back into the room, the players may state the following to each other:

"I've got to Tea-Pot or I'll be late for my appointment"..."I can't figure out how these Tea-Pots are getting into my home"..."I don't like to Tea-Pot but it's sometimes the only way to travel"...etc. When the guesser figures out that "fly" is the secret word which Tea-Pot is taking the place of, whichever player's sentence allowed the guesser to correctly identify the word becomes the guesser in the next game.

Twenty Questions

A player is chosen to be the guesser and leaves the room. Once gone, the other players select an item in the room which the guesser will try to identify upon his/her return. Once the guesser is called back into the room, he/she must try to correctly identify the item by asking no more than twenty questions about it, all of which the answers must be Yes or No. For example, the item to be guessed is a set of keys. The guesser may ask questions such as, "Is it large?", "Is it heavy?", "Does it have a scent?", "Is it useful?", "Can you eat it?", "Does it make a sound?", etc. If the guesser correctly identifies the item within twenty questions, another player then becomes the guesser and the game starts anew. If the guesser cannot identify an item within twenty questions, he/she then leaves the room so the others can select a new item for that same guesser to come back and identify.

Up Jenkins

Players are divided into two teams, which sit across from each other at a table. A captain is selected on each team. We'll call the teams Team A and Team B.

Team A must pass a coin, button, ring or other small item from player to player, everyone's hands remaining under the table so Team B can't see which player currently has the item. The captain of Team B, at any time, may shout "Up Jenkins!" in which all players of Team A must place their hands on the table, fists closed, as if each player is holding the item.

Players on Team B then have to correctly identify who on Team A has the item in their hand. However, only the captain may provide the guess. Team B players would have to unanimously tell the captain who on Team A has the item or if the team's guess is not unanimous and the captain is told of different Team A players holding the item, the captain may say any name his/her teammates have provided. If guessed correctly, Team B wins a point. If guessed incorrectly, Team A wins a point. The teams then swap roles, Team B now being the side hiding the item. The two teams take turns hiding the item and guessing who has it. Captains may be changed in each game as well. This game lasts for as long as player wish. Once it is decided the game should end, whichever team has earned the most points wins the game.

What is My Thought Like?

One player is selected to be the thinker. The thinker must think of a person or object. One by one, the thinker asks the other players what their (the thinker's) thought is of. When all players have said what they believe the thinker's thought is, the thinker then reveals his/her thought. It is likely that none of the players have correctly guessed what the thinker's thought was but they must convince the thinker to believe that what they were thinking can be linked to the thinker's thought.

To demonstrate, the thinker is thinking of a bedsheet. The other players in the game guessed the thinker was thinking of a chair, his mother, and a basket. The player who guessed the chair isn't able to connect it to the bedsheet and therefore receives no point. The next player, who guessed the thinker was thinking of his mother, tries to explain that the thinker's mother can be connected with the bedsheet because the thinker's mother would change the bedding when the thinker was a child. The thinker may consider this response valid and that player earns a point. The next player tries to connect the basket with the bedsheet by saying if the basket is brought on a picnic and a blanket is forgotten, having a bedsheet would be useful to sit on. The thinker may consider this explanation ridiculous and that player receives no point. This continues on until all players have taken their turn at trying to convince the thinker that their item's connection to the bedsheet is valid. A new round of the game then begins. Each player takes turns as the thinker with each new round. Once each player has had the opportunity of being the thinker, the game is over. The player with the most points at the end of the game is the winner.

BAD DAY TO BE
OUTDOORS?

PLAY SOME
PARLOR GAMES!

AND ENJOY ENTERTAINING CONTENT AT
WWW.THEVICTORIANHISTORIAN.COM

Happy Jumps

This was a popular game enjoyed during the Christmas season. Twelve candles are lit and placed in a row on the floor (or in a horseshoe shape around the room if the room is not long large enough to line all candles in a straight row). All candles should be spaced at least two feet apart. Each candle represents a month of the year. The first candle represents January, the second February, the third March and so on. One player then jumps over all twelve candles, one candle at a time. The idea is by jumping over a candle and not extinguishing the flame by doing so, the month represented by that candle will be a happy one in the coming year for that individual. If jumping over a candle extinguishes the flame, the month represented by that candle will be an unpleasant one. If any candle is extinguished by a player, it is relit and the next player then jumps over all twelve candles, these actions being repeated until all players have had the opportunity of jumping over the candles.

Raisin Race

A thread measuring a yard long is strung through a raisin, the raising being positioned at the center of the thread. Two people each take an end of the thread in their mouths and begin chewing it quickly. As the players quickly chew the thread, the raisin will naturally be pulled back and forth in a tug-of-war fashion. Whichever player pulls the raisin into their mouth first will be the first of those two players to be wed.

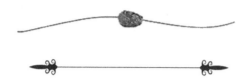

Three Tin Cups

This game was originally played using tin cups but any cup for this game will do. Three cups are partially filled with water, just enough so it won't make a large mess if the cups spill over. Three funnels are placed in a row on the floor about two feet apart, with the narrow ends facing up. The cups of water are balanced on each narrow end of the funnels. One player then jumps over each cup of water, careful not to knock any of them over, whether by accidentally kicking them or creating a vibration upon landing. Anyone who successfully jumps over all three cups without knocking any off the funnels will be married early. Anyone who knocks over one cup will be married at middle age. Anyone who knocks over two cups will be married later in life. Finally, anyone who knocks over all three cups will never be married.

Any cups knocked over are to be refilled with water and replaced on the funnel for the next player to jump over.

Though this game calls for a small amount of water in each cup, it may be played without using water. However, having some water in the cups adds to the caution players take in jumping over them, leading to suspense and excitement.

True Lover Test

This game was originally only played by ladies who were single but single gentlemen may participate as well. Each person takes two hazelnuts and applies a name to each. The names are to be actual names of two people that individual has affections for. The hazelnuts are then placed into hot coal.

If one of the hazelnuts bursts, it indicates the individual whose name was applied to that hazelnut would not be a faithful companion. If the hazelnut does not burst but instead burns with a steady glow and becomes ashes, it indicates that individual would be faithful. If both hazelnuts burst, neither would be faithful. If both burn steadily and turn to ashes, both would make a faithful companion.

TRICKS
DISGUISED
AS GAMES

Boots Without Shoes

The leader of this game will be one of the only players in the room familiar with it, if not the only one familiar with the game. If there happen to be others familiar with this game, they cannot participate but may stay in the room with the game leader. All other players are to leave the room. The game leader sits in a chair and a vacant chair is placed across from him/her. One by one, each player is called in, who will sit in the vacant chair. The game leader will then say, "Say boots without shoes", in which that player sitting across from the game leader will naturally repeat as instructed. However, this is not correct. The game leader will then repeat "Say boots without shoes", possibly putting emphasis on the word "without", to which that player again will repeat, also placing emphasis on "without" as believing to be instructed to do. The trick is for the player to say "boots" without saying "shoes", hence the leader's instruction to "Say boots without shoes". Depending on the infliction the game leader places in his instruction to "Say boots without shoes", it will naturally take some players longer than others to figure out exactly what is being asked of them. Those who eventually come to the realization that only "boots" is to be said may remain in the room with the leader while another player is called in to go through the same challenge. The longer it takes someone to figure out what they are being asked to say, the more entertainment it will provide for those now in on the joke.

Clairvoyant

One person, the clairvoyant, leaves the parlor, going into another room and closing the door behind him/her while all others remain in the parlor. One person in the parlor, unknown to all others, is actually working in cooperation with the clairvoyant as his/her assistant, who will ask the clairvoyant a series of questions about items in the parlor and then ask which of those items is being touched. The clairvoyant, behind a closed door in another room will always answer correctly due to specific wording depicted by the assistant in the example below:

Assistant: "Do you remember how the room is furnished in which we are sitting?"
Clairvoyant: "I do."
Assistant: "Do you remember the color of the chairs?"
Clairvoyant: "I do."
Assistant: "How about the design of the rug?"
Clairvoyant: "I do."
Assistant: "And the vase of flowers?"
Clairvoyant: "I do."
Assistant: "The china in the cabinet?"
Clairvoyant: "I do."
Assistant: "The greeting cards on the mantle?"
Clairvoyant: "I do."
Assistant: "Is there nothing in the room that has escaped your notice?"
Clairvoyant: "Nothing."

The clairvoyant's assistant, whose role, again, is unknown to the others, touches an item in the parlor, the vase of flowers in this example. The assistant then asks what item is being touched to which the clairvoyant will always provide the correct answer. In this case, the clairvoyant, still behind a closed door, will say the vase of flowers is being touched, to the astonishment of all in the parlor.

How is this possible? Look closely at the series of questions the assistant asks the clairvoyant. Notice one of the questions, the one about the vase of flowers, begins with the word "And" while all other questions begin with other words. The assistant is telling the clairvoyant which item is going to be touched by starting that question with the word "And".

The Farmyard

The leader of this game announces that he/she is going to whisper the name of an animal in each person's ear and then give a signal to which everyone imitates the sound that animal makes as loud as they can. This is for no other reason than to have everyone make different animal sounds together. However, the leader only whispers the name of an animal into one person's ear, that of a donkey. In everyone else's ear, the leader whispers not to make any sound at the given signal. Upon the signal being given for everyone to make their animal's sound, only one person makes a sound, that of the loud bray of a donkey, resulting in embarrassment by that one player and laughter among the others.

An Impossible Jump

One person (the challenger) challenges another by saying they don't think that person will be able to jump over a short object placed on the floor, whether a coin, hat, marble, book, etc. Naturally an easy action to perform, that person will accept the challenge.

The challenger then places the object on the floor close to a wall, instructing the individual to jump over the object while facing the wall, the wall in the way making the object impossible to jump over.

Kissing the Candlestick

One person, usually a gentleman by Victorian era customs, challenges a lady to kiss a lit candlestick. Many people would not want to get their face that close to a flame for fear of getting burned, hence the challenge. When the lady moves her face in close to the candlestick to kiss it, the gentleman, in one quick motion, pulls the candlestick away and puts his face in the candlestick's place, causing the lady's lips to meet his, thereby stealing a kiss from her.

Make a Card Dance Upon the Wall

One person (Person A) gives another (Person B) a playing card and tells them if they obey what is being asked, that he/she (Person A) can make the card dance upon the wall. As Person B holds the card up to the wall, Person A directs Person B where to place it, such as "a little to the right, not so far, a bit back to the left, a little higher, a little more to the right, now bring it down a bit", etc. It's possible that after some time, Person B may realize that he/she is the victim of a joke, that by following the steps directed, they are in fact the one making the card "dance upon the wall".

Mesmerizing

One person in the room, the mesmerizer, issues a challenge to anyone else that they can, through mesmerism, prevent any person from rising from a chair alone. Accepting the challenge, an individual sits in a chair and the mesmerizer sits in one close by. The mesmerizer then goes through the motions of waving his/her hands around the individual's head, giving the impression of magic occurring. After a short time, the mesmerizer tells the individual to see if he/she can rise up alone. Upon that individual rising from their chair, the mesmerizer also rises from his/hers simultaneously. As the mesmerizer had stated prior to the challenge beginning, that individual cannot, and has not, risen alone.

Obstacles

Chairs, tables and other types of furniture are placed in various spots within the center of the room. A challenge is then issued for anyone to try to make their way across the room blindfolded without bumping into any of the obstacles. Whoever volunteers for the challenge has two minutes to examine the room and memorize where all the obstacles are located. That person is then led out of the room and blindfolded. While out of the room, all of the furniture is quickly removed so that the room is free of any obstacles. The blindfolded person is then brought back into the room where he/she attempts to make their way across the room, careful not to bump into any of the obstacles they have memorized. Little do they know there are now no obstacles in the way. The blindfolded person will fumble their way across the room attempting to avoid obstacles they believe are still there, leading to much amusement by those watching. Only when the blindfold is removed will that person realize they have been tricked.

The Sorcerer Behind the Screen

This game is nearly identical to "Clairvoyant", the only difference being the item touched is something someone is wearing rather than an item in the room.

One person, the sorcerer, stands behind a screen or door, separating him/herself from the others. One person among those others, unknown to the rest, is the sorcerer's assistant, who will ask the sorcerer a series of questions about someone's clothing or accessories and then ask what item on that individual is being touched. We'll use a lady's necklace in this example. The sorcerer, behind a screen or door, will always answer correctly due to specific wording by the assistant as demonstrated in the example below:

Assistant: "Do you know so-and-so?" (the lady)
Sorcerer: "Yes."
Assistant: "Do you remember what she is wearing?"
Sorcerer: "Yes."
Assistant: "The design of her shirt?"
Sorcerer: "Yes."
Assistant: "Her shoes?"
Sorcerer: "Yes."
Assistant: "And her necklace?"

Sorcerer: "Yes."

Assistant: "How about the color of her purse?"

Sorcerer: "Yes."

Assistant: "Is there nothing so-and-so is wearing or carrying that has
         escaped your notice?"

Sorcerer: "Nothing."

The sorcerer's assistant, whose role, again, is unknown to the others, touches an article of clothing or accessory on so-and-so, in this case her necklace. The assistant then asks what item is being touched to which the sorcerer will always provide the correct answer. In this case, the sorcerer will say the necklace is being touched, to the astonishment of all present.

Just as in "Clairvoyant", one question asked by the assistant, the question regarding the necklace, starts with the word "And" while the other questions do not, letting the sorcerer know which article of clothing or accessory is going to be touched.

Wooden Face

A game leader is selected. That leader tells all other players to close their eyes, or each may be blindfolded, and then positions each player in a line as the following example illustrates:

A gentleman is placed with his back toward a wall or door, not knowing the wall/door is right behind him. A lady is then placed face-to-face with that gentleman. Another gentleman would be placed back-to-back with that lady. Then another lady would be placed face-to-face with that gentleman. This pattern of gentleman-lady-gentleman-lady continues until all players are lined up as such so that every person has someone of the opposite gender behind them except the one whose back is to the wall/door. At the leader's signal, all players (with eyes still closed/blindfolded) are to turn around and kiss the person who is now in front of them, leaving that one person whose back was to the wall/door to turn, and as one source states, "give a kiss (to the wall/door) as tender as those the noise of which he hears", making him/her "Wooden Face".

The following image is not accurate, as the lady should be between the two gentlemen but it still provides a general depiction of how the game is played.

Need a gift for the history enthusiast?

GAMES THAT TIME FORGOT

is a gift which is sure to entertain.
Turn back the hands of time and play
parlor games as they were played in the
19th and early 20th century!

THE END

I hope you've enjoyed reading *Games That Time Forgot* and find this to be a useful guide should indoor entertainment be sought on any given day or evening. One is never too old to play games. Games keep the spirit young and lighthearted. As the author known as Aunt Carrie wrote in her 1867 book, *Popular Pastimes for Field and Fireside; or Amusements for Young and Old*, "Some think it childish and silly to play games. Yet if we would only keep our hearts young and happy, we should retain our youth longer, and love our friends and homes better. A good hearty laugh is wholesome." Or as playwright George Bernard Shaw put it, "We don't stop playing because we grow old; we grow old because we stop playing."

PHOTO CREDITS

Title Page - Home Games for the People; Philip J. Cozans, Publisher; New York, 1855

All title pages - Magic Lantern advertisement; The Ladies Home Journal, June 1905

First "Games That Time Forgot" book advertisement – The Ladies Home Journal, October 1903 (modified image)

The Schoolmaster - Mrs. Pott's Cold Handle Sad Irons trade card, 1880s

The Story Game - Godey's Lady's Book; Louis A. Godey, publisher; November, 1867

First "The Victorian Historian" website advertisement – The Ladies Home Journal, April 1893 (modified image)

Apple and Candle – Combined Public Domain images

Are You There, Moriarty? - Indoor Games for Awkward Moments; Ruth Blakely, George Sully & Co.; New York, 1915

The Blind Feeding the Blind - A Book For a Cook; LP Hubbard, Publisher; Minneapolis, 1905

Blind Man's Buff - Popular Pastimes for Amusement and Instruction; By Henry Davenport Northrup; National Publishing Company; Philadelphia, 1901

Blowing Out the Candle - Every Woman's Encyclopedia; The Amalgamated Press, Publisher; London, 1910

Bullet and Bracelet - What Shall We Do Now?; E.V. Lucas & E. Lucas; Grant Richards, London, 1900

Change Seats - Popular Pastimes for Amusement and Instruction; By Henry Davenport Northrup; National Publishing Company; Philadelphia, 1901

Cotton Flies - Cassell's Book of In-Door Amusements, Card Games, and Fireside Fun; Cassell, Petter, Galpin & Co., Publishers; New York, London, Paris, 1881

Ennui - How to Amuse Yourself and Others: The American Girl's Handy Book; By Lina and Adelia Beard Charles Scribner's Sons, Publisher; New York, 1887

Fan Race - Popular Pastimes for Amusement and Instruction; By Henry Davenport Northrup National Publishing Company; Philadelphia, 1901

Flicking the Cork - The Art of Amusing; By Frank Bellew; Carleton, Publisher; New York, 1866

One-legged Lefties - Good Literature; January 1905

Oranges and Lemons - Popular Pastimes for Amusement and Instruction; By Henry Davenport NorthrupNational Publishing Company; Philadelphia, 1901

Where is Your Letter Going? – The Game of District Messenger Boy game box, 1886

Second "The Victorian Historian" website advertisement – The Ladies Home Journal, May 1897 (modified image)

Laughter – Cabinet card, 1890s, Private collection

Pinch Without Laughing - Book of Parlour Games; Peck & Bliss, Publisher; Philadelphia, 1857

Poor Pussy - Indoor Games for Awkward Moments; Ruth Blakely, George Sully & Co., Publisher; New York, 1915

The Sculptor - Hood's Sarsaparilla Book of Parlor Games; C.I. Hood & Co., Publisher; Lowell, Mass, 1890

Throwing the Smile - The Ladies Home Journal; May 1900

Third "The Victorian Historian" website advertisement – The Ladies Home Journal, September 1898 (modified image)

The Artist's Menagerie - Cassell's Book of In-Door Amusements, Card Games, and Fireside Fun;

Cassell, Petter, Galpin &Co., Publishers; New York, London, Paris, 1881

Retsch's Outlines - What Shall We Do Now?; E.V. Lucas & E. Lucas; Grant Richards, London, 1900

Zoological Competition - Every Woman's Encyclopedia; The Amalgamated Press, Publisher; London, 1910

The Cook Who Does Not Like Peas - Mr. Punch's After-Dinner Stories; Punch Library of Humour; London, 1910

Eyes – Public domain

The Game of Location - Popular Pastimes for Field and Fireside; or Amusements for Young and Old; By Aunt Carrie; Milton Bradley & Co, Publisher; Springfield, Mass, 1867

Hiss and Clap - The American Girl's Handy Book; By D.C. Beard; Charles Scribner's Sons, Publisher; New York, 1893

Pass the Slipper - Popular Pastimes for Amusement and Instruction; By Henry Davenport Northrup

National Publishing Company; Philadelphia, 1901

Shadow Buff – The Illustrated Police News, June 16, 1877 (modified image)

Shouting Proverbs - Stenson & Co. Overcoats trade card, 1890s

Fourth "The Victorian Historian" website advertisement – The Ladies Home Journal, May 1895

Raisin Race – Combined public domain images

An Impossible Jump - The Art of Amusing; By Frank Bellew; Carleton, Publisher; New York, 1866

Kissing the Candlestick - Book of Parlour Games; Peck & Bliss, Publisher; Philadelphia, 1857

Obstacles - Fun for the Household; By Emma J. Gray; Published by the Christian Herald, Bible House; New York, 1897

Sorcerer Behind the Screen - Book of Parlour Games; Peck & Bliss, Publisher; Philadelphia, 1857

Wooden Face - Book of Parlour Games; Peck & Bliss, Publisher; Philadelphia, 1857

The End - Mr. Punch's After-Dinner Stories; Punch Library of Humour; London, 1910

Second "Games That Time Forgot" book advertisement – The Ladies Home Journal, October 1903 (modified image)

BIBLIOGRAPHY

The American Girls Handy Book; How to Amuse Yourself and Others. By Lina Beard and Adelia B. Beard. Charles Scribner's Sons, Publisher. Boston, 1887.

The Art of Amusing. By Frank Bellew. Carleton, Publisher. New York, 1866.

Book of Parlour Games. H.C. Peck & Theo. Bliss, Publishers. Philadelphia, 1857.

Cassell's Book of In-Door Amusements, Card Games, and Fireside Fun. Cassell, Petter, Galpin &Co., Publishers. New York, London, Paris, 1881.

Evening Amusements for Everyone. By Frederick D'Arros Plance. Porter & Coates, Publisher. Philadelphia, 1896.

Every Woman's Encyclopedia. Publisher unknown; London, 1910

Fireside Games; for Winter Evening Amusement. Dick & Fitzgerald, Publishers. New York, 1859.

Fun for the Household. By Emma J. Gray. Published by the Christian Herald, Bible House. New York, 1897.

Games for Everybody. By May C. Hoffman. Dodge Publishing Co. New York, 1905.

Games for Halloween. By Mary E. Blain. Barse & Hopkins, Publishers. New York, 1912.

Home Games for the People. Philip J. Cozans, Publisher. New York, 1855.

Hood's Sarsaparilla Book of Parlor Games; C.I. Hood & Co., Publisher; Lowell, Mass, 1890

How to Behave and How to Amuse: A Handy Manual of Etiquette and Parlor Games. By G.H. Sandison. Published by The Christian Herald. New York, 1895.

Parlor Games for the Wise and Otherwise. By Helen E. Hollister. The Penn Publishing Company. Philadelphia, 1900.

Popular Pastimes for Amusement and Instruction. By Henry Davenport Northrup. National Publishing Company. Philadelphia, 1901.

Popular Pastimes for Field and Fireside; or Amusements for Young and Old; By Aunt Carrie; Milton Bradley & Co, Publisher; Springfield, Mass, 1867

What Shall We Do Now? By E.V. Lucas & E. Lucas. Grant Richards, Publisher. London, 1900.

CPSIA information can be obtained
at www.ICGtesting.com
Printed in the USA
BVHW030357131120
593065BV00010B/549/J

9 781796 062069